IDIOMS
THAT SURPRISE US

FOOD IDIOMS

AND

SAYINGS EXPLAINED

ISBN: 978-83-68391-04-6

All rights are reserved 2025 by Life Style Daily. No part of this publication may be reproduced, stored in a retrieval system or transmitted in any form or by any means, electronic, mechanical, photocopying, recording or otherwise, without prior permission.

TABLE OF CONTENTS

1. The Taste of Language	4
Culinary Metaphors as Reflections of Everyday Life	7
How Culture Shapes Food-Related Idioms	9
2. Food as a Metaphor for Success	11
3. Sweet Metaphors in Idioms	21
4. Expressions Related to Beverages	41
5. Idioms About Food and Emotions	61
6. Animals in food idioms	75
7. Culinary Idioms Related to Time and Action	95
8. Funny and Unusual Culinary Idioms	117
9. Regional Differences in Culinary Idioms	137
10. Tips for Using Idioms in Everyday Conversation	150

1.The Taste of Language

Food is more than just fuel for our bodies—it has been an integral part of culture, daily life, and communication for centuries. Idioms related to food are a perfect example of this. Expressions like "bring home the bacon" or "piece of cake" have entered everyday usage, carrying not just literal meanings but symbolic ones as well. But why is food such a common theme in idioms and sayings? The reasons are deeply rooted in human history, culture, and emotions.

Food as a Universal Experience

No matter where in the world, eating is an experience that unites all people. We eat daily, care about provisions, and celebrate significant moments around the table. Culinary metaphors are easy to understand and their meanings intuitive. Food connects people on a fundamental level, making food-related expressions universally relatable.

Example:

"Bread and butter" – Refers to something essential or indispensable in life, just as bread and butter were once staples of every meal.

The Symbolism of Food in Culture

Food is more than just sustenance—it often symbolizes abundance, success, relationships, or emotions. Across languages and cultures, food-related expressions reflect the values and traditions of different communities.

Example:

"The icing on the cake" – Symbolizes something extra that makes a situation perfect, much like frosting enhances a cake.

Everyday Life and Language

For centuries, food preparation was a central aspect of daily life. Many idioms derive from the kitchen, cooking, or communal meals. In earlier times, preparing food was often time-intensive, and processes like baking, fermenting, or cooking inspired linguistic expressions.

Example:

"Piece of cake" – Refers to something very simple, as baking a cake (especially with simpler recipes of the past) was considered an easy task.

Relationships and Shared Meals

Food is also the cornerstone of social relationships. For centuries, people have gathered around the table, sharing meals, stories, and emotions. Idioms like "chew the fat" (to chat) originate from these moments.

Example:

"Spill the beans" – Likely comes from the practice of using beans for voting in ancient Greece, where spilling them could reveal the results.

History and Cultural Context

Food and culinary idioms reflect historical realities. During times of scarcity, phrases like "not worth a hill of beans" (something of little value) had practical significance. Conversely, in times of prosperity, expressions like "bring home the bacon" became symbols of success.

Example:

"Cry over spilled milk" – Reminds us not to dwell on past mishaps, an important lesson in times when resources were scarce.

Fun Facts: Differences in Culinary Idioms

Different cultures have unique approaches to food-related idioms.

For example:

In Polish, people say "nie mydlić oczu" (don't soap the eyes), while the English equivalent is "don't sugarcoat it."

The American idiom "the big cheese" refers to an important person, whereas in the UK, "top banana" is more commonly used.

Conclusion

As a vital part of our lives, food has inspired countless idioms and sayings that have stood the test of time. They help us express emotions, describe situations, and add color to our everyday speech. Have you ever wondered how food idioms are used in different cultures? Or realized how many you use daily without knowing their origins? This book is your gateway to a fascinating journey through the flavorful world of language.

Notes:

Culinary Metaphors as Reflections of Everyday Life

Metaphors related to food are deeply ingrained in our language, as food has played a vital role in daily life for centuries. During times when meal preparation required more effort than today, many kitchen-related activities became a source of inspiration for idioms. These expressions not only describe reality but also help convey emotions, relationships, and situations in a more vivid and relatable way.

Why Has Food Become a Source of Metaphors?

Food is universal and timeless—regardless of culture or era, everyone interacts with it, making it an ideal reference point in everyday communication. Culinary metaphors are both practical and rich with meanings that are easy to understand and remember.

Examples of Culinary Metaphors in Everyday Life

"Piece of cake"

Meaning: Something very simple.

Origin: In times when baking was a daily activity, making a cake was considered an easy task, especially compared to more complex dishes.

"Bring home the bacon"

Meaning: Earning money, providing for one's household.

Origin: The phrase stems from the tradition of rewarding winners of culinary contests with bacon, which was seen as a symbol of abundance.

"The icing on the cake"

Meaning: Something that makes a good situation even better.

Origin: Frosting was once considered a luxury, added only on special occasions.

"Bread and butter"

Meaning: Basic necessities or one's daily work.

Origin: In many cultures, bread and butter were staples of the diet, symbolizing simplicity and essentiality.

"Food for thought"

Meaning: Something that gives you something to think about.

Origin: This phrase uses food as a metaphor for nourishing the mind, just as food nourishes the body.

How Do Culinary Metaphors Aid Communication?

These metaphors are vivid and easy to understand, making it simpler to convey complex ideas in an accessible way. Expressions like "too many cooks spoil the broth" or "spice things up" help illustrate situations that might otherwise be difficult to describe.

Cultural Differences in Culinary Metaphors

Across languages and cultures, culinary metaphors may share similar meanings but take different forms:

In English, people say "as cool as a cucumber," while in Polish, the equivalent might be "as calm as the sea at dawn."

In Spanish, "estar en su salsa" (to be in one's sauce) means being in one's element, which is akin to the English expression "to be in one's element."

Conclusion

Culinary metaphors are mirrors reflecting our everyday lives, needs, and relationships. These expressions demonstrate how our food-related experiences permeate language, making it richer, more emotional, and universal. They quite literally and figuratively make our speech "taste better."

Notes:

How Culture Shapes Food-Related Idioms

Culture is one of the key factors shaping idioms, including those related to food. Idiomatic expressions reflect the traditions, customs, available ingredients, and historical contexts of a community. What is a familiar metaphor in one culture may be completely foreign in another. Examples of food-related idioms highlight the diversity and richness of cultures around the globe.

How Does Food Reflect Cultural Traditions?

Availability of Ingredients

Food idioms often reference local ingredients and dishes that are characteristic of a specific cuisine. For example:

In English, the idiom "big cheese" refers to an important person, as cheese once symbolized wealth in Europe.

In Polish, the saying "niebo w gębie" ("heaven in the mouth") describes something very tasty, reflecting Poles' love for homemade meals.

Rituals and Customs

In many cultures, food is integral to ceremonies, and idioms reflect these traditions:

In Chinese culture, rice symbolizes life and prosperity, as seen in expressions like "chī mǐ" (吃米), meaning "to eat rice"—a metaphor for sustenance.

In Western culture, "bread and butter" represents life's essentials, as bread was a staple in every meal.

How Does History Shape Culinary Idioms?

Historical events and contexts often find their way into language:

"Don't cry over spilled milk" reminds people not to worry about minor losses. This phrase emerged when milk was a valuable yet easily wasted commodity.

"Egg on your face" originated from English theater, where having eggs thrown at an actor symbolized humiliation.

The Polish idiom "nie mydlić oczu" ("don't soap someone's eyes") refers to deception, illustrating regional differences in metaphorical language.

Idioms as Reflections of Cultural Values

Cultural values influence how food is perceived and used in language:

In cultures that value honesty, idioms like "spill the beans" (to reveal a secret) relate to openness but also to betraying trust.

In societies where food symbolizes hospitality, expressions like "to butter someone up" (to flatter someone) reflect ways of building relationships.

Comparing Culinary Idioms Across Cultures

Interestingly, many cultures have similar idioms but use different ingredients or dishes:

In English, people say "as cool as a cucumber," while in Spanish, the equivalent is "más fresco que una lechuga" (as fresh as a lettuce).

The English "selling like hotcakes" is mirrored in Polish as "sprzedawać się jak świeże bułeczki" (selling like fresh bread rolls).

The Impact of Globalization on Culinary Idioms

Globalization has led to the blending of cultures and idioms. Some food-related expressions, like "piece of cake" or "big cheese," are now understood worldwide. Modern fusion cuisines have further enriched language with new metaphors.

Conclusion

Culinary idioms are a perfect example of how culture shapes language. They reflect our everyday experiences, traditions, and values. Through them, we can not only better understand language but also immerse ourselves in the cultural diversity of the world. Are you ready to explore the taste of language in different corners of the globe?

2. Food as a Metaphor for Success

"Bring Home the Bacon" – Earning a Living

Meaning of the Idiom:

The phrase "bring home the bacon" means earning money to support one's family or securing the means for a livelihood. It is often used to emphasize financial success or the ability to provide for essential needs.

History and Origins:

English Roots:

The idiom originates from medieval English traditions, where prizes in contests, such as races or strength competitions, often included bacon. The winner "brought home the bacon," symbolizing abundance and victory.

Religious Legend:

Another theory ties the phrase to 12th-century England, where the church in Dunmow offered a "flitch of bacon" to any married couple that could prove they had not quarreled for a year and a day.

American Adaptation:

The expression gained popularity in the United States in the early 20th century. In 1906, boxer Joe Gans wrote to his mother before a match, promising to "bring home the bacon," which the press interpreted as a pledge of success.

Examples in Sentences:

"John works overtime to bring home the bacon for his family."

"By landing that big contract, our company really brought home the bacon."

"Her new executive job helps her bring home the bacon far more than her previous role."

Why "Bacon"?

Bacon has long been seen as a symbol of luxury and abundance. In times when meat was a prized commodity, bacon represented wealth and the ability to manage resources effectively.

Cultural Differences:

In Polish, there is no direct equivalent to this idiom, but a similar expression might be "zarabiać na chleb" (earning for bread).

In German, the phrase "die Kohle verdienen" (earning coal) is used to describe earning a living.

Conclusion:

"Bring home the bacon" highlights success in earning money and securing a livelihood. Its colorful history and universal meaning make it a frequently used phrase in both everyday language and literature. This idiom is a perfect example of how culinary metaphors can reflect success in daily life.

Notes:

"Big Cheese" – A Person of Importance

Meaning of the Idiom:

The expression "big cheese" refers to someone of great importance, influence, or high social standing. It is often used to describe leaders, managers, or individuals who hold key roles in an organization or society.

History and Origins:

Colonial India:

The origins of the idiom can be traced back to the 19th century when British slang adopted the word "cheese" to signify something important or excellent. This term came from the Hindi word "chiz" (चीज़), meaning "thing" or "object." British colonizers borrowed this term, and the phrase "the real cheese" began to denote something of the highest quality.

American Adaptation:

In the United States, "cheese" evolved into "big cheese" to describe someone who plays a pivotal role—be it a leader or a highly influential individual.

Examples in Sentences:

"The CEO is the big cheese around here—every decision goes through them."

"After her promotion, she's become the big cheese in the marketing department."

"Everyone was excited to meet the big cheese of the company during the gala dinner."

Why "Cheese"?

In the 19th century, cheese was considered a luxurious product associated with wealth and sophistication. In the idiom, "big cheese" symbolizes someone who is central or dominant, much like cheese often takes center stage in culinary creations.

Cultural Differences:

In Polish, there is no direct equivalent, but similar phrases include "gruba ryba" (big fish) or "ważna szychta" (important figure).

In French, the phrase **"le grand manitou"** (literally, the big chief) serves a similar purpose.

In German, "die große Nummer" (the big number) is often used to describe someone very important.

Related Idioms:

"Top banana" – A synonym for "big cheese" often used to describe the leader of a group or project.

"Head honcho" – A popular American idiom meaning the main person in charge.

Conclusion:

"Big cheese" is a colorful idiom that illustrates how food can serve as a metaphor for social status. Its history reflects cultural and linguistic influences between the British and their colonies, while its meaning remains universal—every society has its "big cheese" who plays a vital role.

Notes:

"The Icing on the Cake" – Something That Makes a Situation Perfect

Meaning of the Idiom:

The phrase "the icing on the cake" refers to something extra that makes a good situation even better. It's used to emphasize that something already satisfying has gained an additional element that makes the whole experience exceptional.

History and Origins:

Culinary Origins:

The idiom originates from a time when icing was a luxury addition to cakes. In the 18th and 19th centuries, sugar was an expensive commodity, so the ability to decorate a cake with icing was a sign of wealth. The cake itself was sufficient, but the icing made it look and taste even better.

Symbolism of the Addition:

Icing became a metaphor for something that improves a situation, although it's not essential on its own.

Examples in Sentences:

"I was already happy with my promotion, but the bonus I received was the icing on the cake."

"The sunny weather during our vacation was the icing on the cake after a perfect trip."

"Winning the championship was great, but being named MVP was really the icing on the cake."

Why "Icing"?

Icing is a symbol of luxury and aesthetics. In the past, making icing was a time-consuming process, and cakes decorated with it were reserved for special occasions. Much like in the idiom, something basic—like a success or achievement—gets "decorated" with something additional and exceptional.

Cultural Differences:

In Polish, the expression has a similar meaning: "wisienka na torcie" (cherry on the cake). While it refers to a different decorative element, the meaning remains the same.

In German, the idiom "das Sahnehäubchen" (a dollop of cream on top) also describes something that adds charm or value.

In French, people say "la cerise sur le gâteau" (the cherry on the cake), which is similar to the Polish equivalent.

Related Idioms:

"Cherry on top" – An English equivalent of the Polish "wisienka na torcie", often used interchangeably with "the icing on the cake".

"Gravy" – In the context of something added to something good, for example, "everything else is gravy" means that everything additional is just a bonus.

Examples in Everyday Situations:

Work: "Being invited to the conference was great, and meeting my idol was the icing on the cake."

Relationships: "The dinner itself was wonderful, but the surprise at the end was truly the icing on the cake."

Sports Successes: "Winning the title was amazing for the team, and the reception from the fans after the match was the icing on the cake."

Conclusion:

"The icing on the cake" is an idiom that perfectly captures how small, additional elements can elevate a situation. Its culinary roots and universal meaning make it popular in both everyday language and literature.

Have Your Cake and Eat It Too" – Wanting to Have It All

Meaning of the Idiom:

The phrase "have your cake and eat it too" refers to the desire to have two things that are mutually exclusive—wanting to eat the cake (which consumes it and makes it unavailable) while also keeping it. It's used to describe people who want to enjoy the benefits of two situations at the same time, even when it's impossible.

History and Origins:

Early Usage in Literature:

The first known use of this idiom dates back to the 16th century. It appeared in a 1538 letter written by Thomas, Duke of Norfolk, to King Henry VIII: "a man cannot have his cake and eat it too."

Evolution of the Phrase:

The original meaning pointed to the impossibility of simultaneously possessing and consuming something. Over time, the phrase took on a metaphorical meaning, symbolizing human greed or unrealistic expectations.

Popularity:

The idiom gained widespread popularity in the 20th century, especially in English-speaking countries, where it is used to describe situations in which someone tries to gain more than is feasible.

Examples in Sentences:

"You can't save all your money and go on luxury vacations—you can't have your cake and eat it too."

"He wants the freedom of being single but also the comfort of a committed relationship—he's trying to have his cake and eat it too."

"Trying to work full-time and start a new business on the side is like trying to have your cake and eat it too."

Culinary Analogy:

Imagine a cake—you can admire its appearance and enjoy having it, but once you start eating it, it's no longer whole. This simple image perfectly illustrates the human desire to "have it all," even when it defies the nature of reality.

Cultural Differences:

Polish: The equivalent phrase is "zjeść ciastko i mieć ciastko" (to eat the cake and still have it), carrying the same meaning of impossibility.

French: "Vouloir le beurre et l'argent du beurre" (wanting the butter and the money for the butter), which is equally vivid.

German: The idiom "die Eierlegende Wollmilchsau" (a pig that lays eggs, gives milk, and produces wool) describes someone wanting everything at once.

Related Idioms:

"You can't have it both ways" – Referring to the necessity of choosing between two mutually exclusive options.

"Bite off more than you can chew" – Attempting to do too much at once, often leading to failure.

Examples from Everyday Life:

Work: "You want shorter work hours but a higher salary? Unfortunately, you can't have your cake and eat it too."

Relationships: "You can't expect your partner to be perfect in everything— that's like trying to have your cake and eat it too."

Shopping: "Buying a cheap phone but expecting high quality is like wanting to have your cake and eat it too."

"Chew the Fat" – Casual Conversation

Meaning of the Idiom:

The expression "chew the fat" refers to a relaxed, informal conversation about light, inconsequential topics. It can be translated as "to chat" or "to have a friendly talk." It's commonly used to describe friendly discussions in a laid-back atmosphere.

History and Origins:

Maritime Roots:

The idiom originates from the days of long sea voyages when sailors would chew on salted fat (such as fatty meat or lard) as part of their preserved food supplies. While doing so, they would engage in conversations to pass the time.

Family Context:

During colonial times, fat and cracklings were popular food staples, and chewing them became a metaphor for long conversations shared around the family table.

Evolution of the Idiom:

By the 20th century, the phrase shifted to a more metaphorical meaning, referring to casual conversations, no longer tied to actual eating.

Examples in Sentences:

"We spent the afternoon chewing the fat about our childhood memories."

"After dinner, everyone gathered in the living room to chew the fat and catch up."

"I bumped into an old friend at the cafe, and we ended up chewing the fat for hours."

Why "Fat"?

Fat symbolizes something that can be chewed on for a long time—both literally and metaphorically. In the context of conversation, it represents topics that are light and easy to stretch out, much like chewing on fatty food.

Cultural Differences:

Polish: Similar expressions include "ucinać pogawędkę" (having a chat) or "plotkować" (gossiping).

Spanish: The phrase "echar una charla" refers to having an informal talk.

German: A comparable term might be "quatschen" (chatter about nothing).

Related Idioms:

"Shoot the breeze" – A very similar idiom meaning to engage in a light, aimless conversation.

"Talk shop" – Refers to informal discussions about work or shared professional matters.

Examples from Everyday Life:

Meeting Friends: "After lunch, we stayed a bit longer to chew the fat about recent events."

Relaxing After Work: "Every evening at the office, they gather together to chew the fat before heading home."

Family Time: "We love sitting by the fireplace and chewing the fat with our grandparents about the old days."

Conclusion:

"Chew the fat" captures the essence of relaxing moments spent in casual conversation. Its historical roots in maritime life and culinary traditions highlight how language evolves by drawing inspiration from everyday experiences. This phrase perfectly conveys the warmth and camaraderie of informal chats.

3. Sweet Metaphors in Idioms

"Sweeten the Deal" – Making an Offer More Attractive

Meaning of the Idiom:

The phrase "sweeten the deal" refers to adding something extra or beneficial to a proposal to make it more appealing and harder to refuse. This idiom is often used in the context of negotiations, business deals, or situations where someone seeks to persuade the other party by offering additional advantages.

History and Origins:

Culinary Roots:

The verb "sweeten" comes from the practice of adding sugar or honey to food to enhance its flavor. Over time, the act of "sweetening" became a metaphor for making something more enjoyable or attractive.

Rise in Popularity:

The idiom gained prominence in the 20th century, especially in business and sales contexts. Its clarity and simplicity quickly made it a part of everyday language.

Examples in Sentences:

"The company sweetened the deal by offering a signing bonus with the job."

"To close the sale, the car dealer sweetened the deal with free servicing for a year."

"They sweetened the deal by including an extra month's rent-free period in the lease agreement."

Cultural Context:

In American English, this idiom is particularly popular in business, sales, and negotiations. It also finds its way into everyday scenarios where someone attempts to make an offer more enticing by including additional perks.

Related Idioms:

"Throw in a little extra" – To add something additional to increase value or attractiveness.

"Seal the deal" – To finalize or conclude an agreement.

Examples from Daily Life:

In Business Negotiations:

"The supplier agreed to sweeten the deal by offering a 10% discount on bulk orders."

In Real Estate:

"The landlord sweetened the deal by including free parking in the rental agreement."

In Personal Relationships:

"He sweetened the deal by offering to take care of the chores if she agreed to his plans for the weekend."

Conclusion:

"Sweeten the deal" is a vivid idiom that highlights the art of persuasion through small but impactful additional benefits. Its culinary origins and broad applicability make it a versatile phrase used in both professional and casual conversations.

Notes:

"Sugarcoat" – To Soften Something Difficult to Accept

Meaning of the Idiom:

The term "sugarcoat" means presenting something difficult, unpleasant, or negative in a more palatable, gentle, or acceptable way. It is often used when someone tries to soften bad news or an uncomfortable truth to make it easier to hear or accept.

History and Origins:

Culinary Reference:

The word "sugarcoat" literally means covering something with sugar to improve its taste. Historically, bitter medicines were often coated with sugar to make them easier to swallow.

Metaphorical Meaning:

Over time, the term evolved to be used metaphorically, referring to the act of presenting unpleasant truths in a way that is more appealing or less harsh.

Examples in Sentences:

"The manager didn't sugarcoat the feedback; he was honest about the mistakes."

"She tried to sugarcoat the bad news, but it was still difficult to hear."

"Politicians often sugarcoat their policies to make them more appealing to the public."

Cultural Context:

In American culture, the idiom "sugarcoat" is commonly used in discussions about politics, workplace communication, or personal relationships. It often refers to attempts to cushion the blow or make negative information sound less severe.

Related Idioms:

"Put a spin on it" – Presenting information in a favorable light, often manipulatively.

"Soft-pedal" – Downplaying the importance or seriousness of something to make it seem less significant.

Examples from Everyday Life:

Workplace:

"The HR department sugarcoated the announcement about layoffs by emphasizing the support packages."

Relationships:

"He didn't sugarcoat the truth about why their relationship wasn't working."

Parenting:

"Parents often sugarcoat difficult topics when explaining them to young children."

Conclusion:

"Sugarcoat" is a versatile idiom that vividly captures the act of softening harsh truths. Its origins in culinary practices and its metaphorical evolution illustrate how language draws from everyday experiences to create relatable expressions. This phrase is widely used across professional and personal contexts, making it a valuable tool for communicating delicately.

"Honey-Tongued" – Sweet Words That May Be Deceptive

Meaning of the Idiom:

"Honey-tongued" refers to a person who speaks in a sweet, polite, and persuasive manner, often with the intent to manipulate or conceal their true motives. While it can describe eloquence, it also carries a warning that such words might not be entirely sincere.

History and Origins:

Symbolism of Honey:

Honey has long been associated with sweetness, pleasure, and allure. The combination of "honey" and "tongued" forms a metaphor for someone whose words are as sweet as honey but may lack honesty.

Literary References:

The phrase appeared in English literature as early as the 16th century, often to praise beautiful speech or to caution against flattery. Shakespeare used similar language to describe individuals whose sweet words might mask deceit.

Examples in Sentences:

"The honey-tongued politician charmed the audience, but many doubted his sincerity."

"She has a honey-tongued way of convincing people, even when her intentions aren't pure."

"Beware of honey-tongued flattery; it often hides ulterior motives."

Cultural Context:

In Anglo-Saxon culture, the idiom "honey-tongued" is frequently used in literature and everyday conversations to warn against people who speak beautifully but may not be trustworthy. It is particularly common in contexts like politics, marketing, and personal relationships, where words are powerful tools of persuasion.

Related Idioms:

"Silver-tongued" – Describes someone who is eloquent and persuasive, but not necessarily sincere.

"Smooth talker" – Refers to someone who speaks charmingly, often with manipulative intent.

Examples from Everyday Life:

Politics:

"The honey-tongued candidate promised change, but his actions spoke otherwise."

Business:

"The sales representative's honey-tongued pitch made the product sound perfect, but it didn't live up to the claims."

Relationships:

"He was honey-tongued when they first met, but she soon realized he wasn't trustworthy."

Conclusion:

"Honey-tongued" is a vivid idiom that highlights the dual nature of eloquence—words can be sweet and persuasive, yet sometimes conceal hidden motives. Its historical roots and literary connections emphasize the timelessness of this concept, making it a relevant cautionary term in both professional and personal interactions.

"As Easy as Pie" – Something Very Simple

Meaning of the Idiom:

"As easy as pie" refers to something extremely simple or easy to do. This phrase is used to emphasize that a task or activity requires little effort or skill.

History and Origins:

American Roots:

The idiom originated in the United States and gained popularity in the early 20th century. It refers to the pleasure of eating pie, which was seen as a symbol of simple, homely comfort. At the time, baking a pie was considered a basic and straightforward task in American culture, contributing to the idiom's metaphorical meaning.

Literary Use:

The phrase began appearing in American novels and newspapers, describing tasks that are both enjoyable and easy.

Examples in Sentences:

"Solving that math problem was as easy as pie for her."

"Don't worry about the application process—it's as easy as pie."

"Once you learn the steps, cooking this dish will be as easy as pie."

Cultural Context:

The idiom "as easy as pie" is popular in American culture, where pies hold symbolic and emotional significance. They are associated with the simplicity of rural life, tradition, and comfort. The expression is used in both formal and informal settings to convey ease.

Related Idioms in English:

"Piece of cake" – A very similar phrase meaning something easy and enjoyable.

"No sweat" – Emphasizing that something is not difficult or effortful.

Examples from Everyday Life:

Learning:

"For someone who loves technology, setting up the new phone was as easy as pie."

Work:

"After years of practice, writing reports is as easy as pie for her."

Sports:

"For a professional swimmer, crossing the pool was as easy as pie."

Conclusion:

"As easy as pie" is a classic idiom that highlights the simplicity and ease of a task. Its origins in American culture reflect the symbolic association of pie with comfort and straightforwardness. This expression remains widely used to describe tasks that are both manageable and enjoyable.

Notes:

"Apple of One's Eye" – Someone Cherished

Meaning of the Idiom:

The phrase "apple of one's eye" refers to a person or thing that is highly valued, deeply loved, or extremely important to someone. It is used to express strong affection or attachment to a favorite person, pet, or even an idea.

History and Origins:

Ancient Roots:

The expression originates from Old English, where "apple" referred to the pupil of the eye. The pupil was considered precious because it allowed sight. Thus, the metaphor "apple of one's eye" came to signify something deeply treasured and protected.

Biblical References:

The idiom appears in the Bible, in both the Old and New Testaments, symbolizing God's care and love for His people.

Modern Usage:

The contemporary meaning of the idiom solidified in the 19th century and remains widely used today.

Examples in Sentences:

"His daughter is the apple of his eye; he'd do anything for her."

"That classic car is the apple of his eye—he spends every weekend polishing it."

"The little puppy quickly became the apple of the family's eye."

Cultural Context:

In English-speaking cultures, the idiom "apple of one's eye" carries a warm and emotional tone. It is often used in familial contexts, particularly by parents to describe their children, but it can also apply to cherished possessions or beloved pets.

Related Idioms in English:

"Someone's pride and joy" – Something or someone that brings immense pride and happiness.

"The light of one's life" – A person who is the center of someone's world.

Examples from Everyday Life:

Family:

"Her youngest son has always been the apple of her eye."

Hobbies:

"The painting he created last summer is the apple of his eye."

Pets:

"Their golden retriever is clearly the apple of their eye—they spoil him rotten."

Conclusion:

"Apple of one's eye" is a timeless idiom that conveys deep affection and admiration. Its historical roots in vision and protection reflect how language evolves to express profound emotional connections. This phrase remains an enduring way to describe someone or something of utmost importance.

Notes:

"Have a Finger in the Pie" – To Be Involved in Something

Meaning of the Idiom:

The phrase <u>"have a finger in the pie"</u> means being involved in or having a share in multiple activities, projects, or situations. It often describes someone actively participating in various endeavors—sometimes excessively so.

History and Origins:

Culinary Reference:

The idiom originates from the imagery of someone literally sticking a finger into different pies, symbolizing curiosity and a desire for control or involvement.

Early Usage:

The expression first appeared in English literature in the 16th century. Initially, it referred to meddling in others' affairs, but over time, it expanded to describe general involvement or participation.

Evolution of Meaning:

Over time, the phrase came to describe people who influence or engage with multiple areas of life or business, often with overzealous involvement.

Examples in Sentences:

"She has a finger in the pie of almost every committee at work."

"The CEO likes to have a finger in the pie of every major decision in the company."

"He always has a finger in the pie when it comes to planning community events."

Cultural Context:

In English-speaking cultures, this idiom frequently appears in business and social contexts. It can carry either a positive or negative connotation depending on the situation—praising someone's engagement or criticizing their tendency to interfere in too many matters.

Related Idioms in English:

"Too many irons in the fire" – Describes being involved in too many activities simultaneously.

"Spread oneself too thin" – Refers to attempting too many things at once, often leading to lower-quality work.

Examples from Everyday Life:

Work:

"The manager has a finger in the pie of every department—it's hard to get anything done without her approval."

Politics:

"He's a skilled diplomat who always seems to have a finger in the pie during important negotiations."

Community:

"The volunteer organization thrives because so many people have a finger in the pie."

Conclusion:

"Have a finger in the pie" is a versatile idiom that vividly captures the idea of involvement and influence. Whether it highlights active engagement or meddling, its roots in culinary imagery and its historical evolution make it a widely used and relatable expression in both professional and personal contexts.

Notes:

"A Spoonful of Sugar" – Helpful Support in Difficult Situations

Meaning of the Idiom:

"A spoonful of sugar" refers to a small gesture that makes a difficult or unpleasant situation more bearable. The phrase suggests that adding something positive or uplifting can help ease challenges.

History and Origins:

Culinary Reference:

The idiom originates from the practice of adding sugar to bitter medicine to make it easier to swallow. This serves as a vivid metaphor for softening difficulties in daily life.

Popularity Through Culture:

The phrase gained widespread recognition thanks to the song "A Spoonful of Sugar" from Disney's Mary Poppins (1964). In the film, it implies that even the most unpleasant tasks can become manageable with the right attitude and a touch of positivity.

Examples in Sentences:

"The teacher used a spoonful of sugar by turning the lesson into a fun game."

"He offered a spoonful of sugar by bringing her favorite snacks to the long meeting."

"Adding a bit of humor was like a spoonful of sugar that eased the tension in the room."

Cultural Context:

In American culture, this idiom is commonly used in contexts where people face challenges, particularly in interpersonal relationships, work, or parenting. It carries a positive connotation, encouraging creative ways to improve difficult circumstances.

Related Idioms in English:

<u>"Make the best of it"</u> – To handle a difficult situation as well as possible.

<u>"Lighten the mood"</u> – To make a tense atmosphere more relaxed.

Examples from Everyday Life:

Parenting:

"Getting kids to do their chores can be hard, but singing songs is like a spoonful of sugar that makes it fun."

Work:

"She eased the stress of a busy day with a spoonful of sugar—a quick coffee break for the team."

Relationships:

"During the argument, he added a spoonful of sugar by reminding her of their happy memories."

Conclusion:

"A spoonful of sugar" is a heartwarming idiom that highlights the power of small positive actions to alleviate difficulty. Its roots in both culinary traditions and popular culture have made it a universally recognized expression of optimism and resilience.

Notes:

"Like Taking Candy from a Baby" – Something Extremely Easy

Meaning of the Idiom:

The phrase "like taking candy from a baby" refers to a task or situation that is exceptionally easy to accomplish. It often carries a connotation of being so simple that it feels almost unethical, as taking candy from a baby requires no effort but could be seen as cruel.

History and Origins:

Vivid Metaphor:

The idiom draws on the simplicity of an adult taking candy from a child—a child cannot defend themselves, highlighting how little effort is needed to achieve the goal.

First Usage:

The phrase emerged in the English language during the 19th century, appearing in literature and casual speech. It initially described very easy victories or achievements.

Examples in Sentences:

"Convincing him to agree to the deal was like taking candy from a baby."

"The opposing team was so unprepared that winning the match felt like taking candy from a baby."

"Fixing the broken chair was like taking candy from a baby for someone with his skills."

Cultural Context:

In American culture, this idiom is used in both positive and negative contexts. Positively, it emphasizes how simple it was to succeed, while negatively, it can imply a lack of ethics or fairness in a situation where one side had an overwhelming advantage.

Related Idioms in English:

"A walk in the park" – Describes something very easy to accomplish.

"Piece of cake" – Refers to an easy and enjoyable task.

Examples from Everyday Life:

Work:

"Writing the report was like taking candy from a baby; I've done it so many times before."

Sports:

"Beating the amateur player felt like taking candy from a baby for the professional champion."

Daily Life:

"Getting her to agree to a coffee date was like taking candy from a baby—she loves coffee."

Conclusion:

"Like taking candy from a baby" is a vivid idiom that highlights the ease of a task or accomplishment. While it conveys simplicity, its underlying metaphor of imbalance can also imply a moral consideration, making it versatile for various contexts.

Notes:

"Too Many Cooks Spoil the Broth" – Too Many People Can Ruin Something

Meaning of the Idiom:

The phrase "too many cooks spoil the broth" means that involving too many people in a single task or project can lead to chaos, conflicts, or inefficiency. It highlights that an excess of input and actions can have the opposite of the intended effect.

History and Origins:

Culinary Roots:

The idiom originates from the kitchen, where having too many cooks working on one dish, especially a delicate broth, can result in inconsistent flavors or even spoil the meal. "Broth" is used as a metaphor for tasks requiring precision and harmony.

First Usage:

The phrase appeared in the English language as early as the 16th century and was used as a cautionary saying against excessive involvement.

Examples in Sentences:

"The project failed because too many cooks spoiled the broth—everyone wanted to do things their way."

"We don't need more opinions on this design; too many cooks will spoil the broth."

"Planning the wedding became stressful because too many cooks were spoiling the broth."

Cultural Context:

In English-speaking cultures, this idiom is often used in the context of teamwork, group projects, or event planning. It serves as a warning against a lack of centralized leadership or having too many individuals attempting to manage a single endeavor.

Related Idioms in English:

"Too many chiefs and not enough Indians" – Describes a situation where there are too many leaders and not enough workers to carry out the task.

"A camel is a horse designed by committee" – Suggests that group decision-making can lead to impractical or strange results.

Examples from Everyday Life:

Work:

"The presentation wasn't coherent because too many cooks spoiled the broth—everyone added their own slides."

Family:

"The family dinner got complicated because too many cooks spoiled the broth in the kitchen."

Community:

"Organizing the festival would've been smoother if fewer people were involved—too many cooks spoiled the broth."

Conclusion:

"Too many cooks spoil the broth" is a timeless idiom that emphasizes the importance of clear leadership and streamlined collaboration. Its roots in culinary practices provide a vivid metaphor for the dangers of over-involvement, making it a widely understood expression in both professional and personal contexts.

"The Cherry on Top" – A Small Extra Detail That Enhances Something

Meaning of the Idiom:

"The cherry on top" refers to a minor, additional element that makes a good situation or achievement even better. The phrase emphasizes that something already satisfying has gained extra value or appeal.

History and Origins:

Culinary Roots:

The idiom originates from desserts, such as ice cream sundaes, where a cherry on top symbolizes luxury and completion. While not necessary, the cherry adds visual and flavorful charm, becoming a metaphor for improving a situation with a small but impactful touch.

Spread of the Idiom:

The phrase became widely used in the 20th century, especially in the United States, and quickly gained popularity in personal, professional, and social contexts.

Examples in Sentences:

"Winning the lottery was amazing, but getting a vacation included was the cherry on top."

"The team worked hard on the project, and the client's positive feedback was the cherry on top."

"She already had a great day, and the surprise gift from her friend was just the cherry on top."

Cultural Context:

The idiom "the cherry on top" is widely used in American culture in both formal and informal settings. It often describes positive situations enhanced by an additional gesture, reward, or circumstance.

Related Idioms in English:

"The icing on the cake" – A very similar phrase, referring to something that makes a good situation even better.

"Finishing touch" – A small detail that completes something perfectly.

Examples from Everyday Life:

Work:

"Completing the project ahead of schedule was great, but the bonus payment was the cherry on top."

Relationships:

"Their date was perfect, and the sunset walk was the cherry on top."

Sports:

"Winning the championship was amazing, and the standing ovation from the crowd was the cherry on top."

Conclusion:

"The cherry on top" is a delightful idiom that highlights how small, extra touches can elevate an already positive situation. Its origins in culinary traditions provide a vivid metaphor for enhancement, making it a versatile expression for both everyday and professional conversations.

4. Expressions Related to Beverages

"Not My Cup of Tea" – Something That Doesn't Appeal to Me

Meaning of the Idiom:

"Not my cup of tea" refers to something that doesn't match one's tastes, interests, or preferences. The phrase is used to politely express dislike or disinterest in something.

History and Origins:

British Roots:

The idiom originates from British culture, where tea symbolizes comfort and enjoyment. By the 19th century, the phrase "my cup of tea" was used to describe something that brought joy or satisfaction. Its opposite meaning, "not my cup of tea," gained popularity in the 20th century as a polite way to express disapproval.

Examples in Sentences:

"I know hiking is popular, but it's not my cup of tea."

"He enjoys watching horror movies, but they're not my cup of tea."

"Cooking elaborate meals every day is not my cup of tea—I prefer something simple."

Cultural Context:

The idiom "not my cup of tea" is particularly popular in the UK and other English-speaking countries. It is commonly used in informal conversations, as well as in formal contexts, as a subtle and polite way to express differing opinions.

Related Idioms in English:

"Not my thing" – A more modern and informal version of the idiom.

"To each their own" – A phrase that acknowledges the diversity of tastes and preferences.

Examples from Everyday Life:

Hobbies:

"He loves gardening, but it's not my cup of tea—I prefer indoor activities."

Food:

"Spicy food is not my cup of tea; I prefer milder flavors."

Entertainment:

"Romantic comedies are not my cup of tea, but I'll watch them if you want."

Notes:

"Storm in a Teacup" – Making a Big Deal Out of a Small Problem

Meaning of the Idiom:

"Storm in a teacup" refers to an exaggerated reaction to a small or insignificant issue. The idiom is used to describe situations where someone makes a big fuss over something trivial.

History and Origins:

British Origin:

The phrase is popular in Britain and alludes to the idea that a storm inside a small vessel like a teacup couldn't possibly be significant, symbolizing the overreaction to a minor issue.

Roman Roots:

The earliest known version of this expression comes from the Roman writer Cicero, who used the Latin phrase "excitatio fluctus in simpulo" (stirring waves in a ladle). Over time, this idea was adapted into English.

Examples in Sentences:

"Their argument about the seating arrangement was just a storm in a teacup."

"I can't believe they're so upset about a typo—it's really a storm in a teacup."

"The media turned the minor issue into a storm in a teacup, exaggerating its importance."

Cultural Context:

The idiom "storm in a teacup" is especially popular in Britain, where tea holds cultural significance. Its American counterpart is "tempest in a teapot," which conveys the same idea of blowing a small problem out of proportion.

Related Idioms in English:

"Make a mountain out of a molehill" – A very similar phrase meaning to exaggerate a small problem.

"Blow something out of proportion" – Describes an overreaction to a minor issue.

Examples from Everyday Life:

Workplace:

"The email miscommunication caused a storm in a teacup among the team."

Family:

"Their disagreement over who should do the dishes turned into a storm in a teacup."

Media:

"The debate about the celebrity's outfit was just a storm in a teacup blown up by social media."

Conclusion:

"Storm in a teacup" is a vivid idiom that captures the tendency to overreact to trivial matters. Its cultural roots in both Britain and ancient Rome highlight the timeless nature of this behavior, making it a relatable and widely used expression in both professional and personal contexts.

Notes:

"Spill the Tea" – Gossiping

Meaning of the Idiom:

"Spill the tea" refers to sharing gossip, secret information, or juicy details about others. It's often used to encourage someone to reveal something interesting or sensational.

History and Origins:

Modern Roots:

The phrase became popular in American slang, particularly within LGBTQ+ communities and drag culture in the 1990s. It later gained widespread recognition through internet memes and entertainment shows like "RuPaul's Drag Race."

Symbolism of Tea (Tea):

In this context, "tea" is shorthand for "truth," implying the act of sharing the truth, often in the form of gossip or candid opinions.

Examples in Sentences:

"Come on, spill the tea—what happened at the party last night?"

"I heard you know something about their breakup. Spill the tea!"

"She always knows all the gossip and loves to spill the tea during lunch."

Cultural Context:

"Spill the tea" is now widely used in pop culture, social media, and informal conversations, particularly among younger generations. The phrase is playful and humorous, often referring to gossip about celebrities, friends, or social events.

Related Idioms in English:

"Dish the dirt" – A very similar phrase meaning to share gossip.

"Give the lowdown" – To reveal detailed information about something.

Examples from Everyday Life:

Friends:

"You look excited! Spill the tea—what's the big news?"

Social Media:

"The influencer promised to spill the tea about the drama with her collaborator."

Work Gossip:

"He always spills the tea about what's happening in the office."

Conclusion:

"Spill the tea" is a modern idiom that captures the playful and social nature of sharing gossip. Its origins in LGBTQ+ and drag culture have enriched its association with wit and humor, making it a popular expression in today's informal conversations and digital culture.

Notes:

"Milk of Human Kindness" – Human Compassion

Meaning of the Idiom:

"Milk of human kindness" refers to natural human goodness, compassion, and care for others. The phrase highlights traits like empathy, generosity, and a willingness to help, which are seen as fundamental aspects of human nature.

History and Origins:

Shakespearean Roots:

The idiom originates from William Shakespeare's tragedy Macbeth (1606). In the play, Lady Macbeth says of her husband: "Yet do I fear thy nature; It is too full o' the milk of human kindness." In this context, the phrase suggests that Macbeth is too compassionate and kind to kill the king and seize power.

Evolution of Meaning:

Over time, the phrase evolved into a more positive expression, symbolizing human goodness and altruism.

Examples in Sentences:

"She showed the milk of human kindness by helping the homeless man find a place to stay."

"Volunteering at the shelter is a true example of the milk of human kindness."

"His generous donation to the charity was a reflection of the milk of human kindness."

Cultural Context:

The idiom is more formal and literary, often used in descriptions of charitable actions, humanitarian efforts, or extraordinary acts of kindness. In English-speaking cultures, it underscores the belief that kindness is an intrinsic part of human nature, though it sometimes requires nurturing or emphasis.

Related Idioms in English:

"Heart of gold" – Refers to someone with a very kind and generous heart.

"Good Samaritan" – Describes a person who helps others, especially strangers, out of the goodness of their heart.

Examples from Everyday Life:

Charity:

"Her decision to donate her time and money to the orphanage is driven by the milk of human kindness."

Community:

"In times of crisis, you can see the milk of human kindness in how neighbors help each other."

Personal Relationships:

"His patience and understanding show the milk of human kindness in every interaction."

Conclusion:

"Milk of human kindness" is a timeless idiom that captures the essence of human empathy and generosity. Its Shakespearean origins lend it a formal and literary tone, making it a powerful expression for highlighting acts of altruism and care in both personal and societal contexts.

"Cry Over Spilled Milk" – Worrying About Something That Can't Be Changed

Meaning of the Idiom:

"Cry over spilled milk" refers to complaining or worrying about something that has already happened and cannot be undone. The idiom suggests that such behavior is unproductive and encourages focusing on the future rather than dwelling on the past.

History and Origins:

Early Usage:

The phrase originated in 17th-century England, where milk symbolized a basic and valuable commodity. The first recorded reference appeared in 1659 in an essay by James Howell, who wrote: "No weeping for shed milk."

Simplicity of the Metaphor:

Spilled milk was seen as a loss, but one that couldn't be recovered, making it a perfect metaphor for irreversible situations.

Examples in Sentences:

"I know you're upset about the mistake, but there's no use crying over spilled milk now."

"We lost the game, but it's no time to cry over spilled milk—let's focus on the next one."

"The vase is broken, but crying over spilled milk won't fix it."

Cultural Context:

This idiom is widely used in English-speaking cultures, both in everyday conversations and in literature or media. It emphasizes the importance of accepting things that cannot be changed and focusing on solutions or future actions.

Related Idioms in English:

"What's done is done" – Stresses that the past cannot be altered.

"Let bygones be bygones" – Advises letting go of past grievances or regrets.

Examples from Everyday Life:

Work:

"The deadline was missed, but there's no point crying over spilled milk—let's focus on the next project."

Family:

"I burned the cookies, but crying over spilled milk won't bake a new batch."

Relationships:

"He forgot their anniversary, but instead of crying over spilled milk, she planned a makeup dinner."

Conclusion:

"Cry over spilled milk" is a practical idiom that encourages resilience and forward-thinking. Its origins in everyday life make it relatable and timeless, reminding us to accept the past and concentrate on what can still be changed.

Notes:

"Brew a Storm" – Creating Conflicts

Meaning of the Idiom:

"Brew a storm" refers to actions that lead to escalating tensions, conflicts, or problems. The phrase describes situations where someone, intentionally or unintentionally, provokes a storm of emotions or difficulties that can spiral out of control.

History and Origins:

Culinary Roots:

The term "brew" comes from the process of preparing beverages like tea or coffee, where ingredients gradually mix and intensify. In the idiom, this process symbolizes the buildup of problems or emotions until they reach a critical point.

Metaphorical Significance of Storms:

In English literature and language, storms often symbolize chaos and conflict, making them an ideal metaphor for situations where small issues snowball into significant problems.

Examples in Sentences:

"Her constant complaints brewed a storm among the team members."

"Spreading false rumors is a surefire way to brew a storm in any community."

"His insensitive comments brewed a storm on social media."

Cultural Context:

The idiom "brew a storm" is widely used in English-speaking cultures, particularly in contexts involving interpersonal relationships, workplace disputes, or social media controversies. It is often used as a cautionary expression to warn against actions that might escalate problems.

Related Idioms in English:

"Add fuel to the fire" – To intensify an existing conflict or problem.

"Rock the boat" – To cause disturbance in an otherwise stable situation.

Examples from Everyday Life:

Workplace:

"By criticizing the management during the meeting, he brewed a storm that disrupted the entire team."

Family:

"She brewed a storm by bringing up an old argument during the family dinner."

Media:

"The journalist's controversial article brewed a storm of public outrage."

Conclusion:

"Brew a storm" is a dynamic idiom that vividly captures the gradual buildup of conflict and chaos. Its roots in culinary practices and the metaphor of storms make it a powerful expression for describing the consequences of provocative actions, both intentional and unintentional.

Notes:

"As Flat as a Pancake" – Something Very Flat

Meaning of the Idiom:

"As flat as a pancake" describes something exceptionally flat, with no height or elevation. The phrase is used both literally and metaphorically, such as to describe landscapes, objects, or situations lacking impact or dynamism.

History and Origins:

Culinary Reference:

The idiom refers to traditional pancakes, known for their thin and flat shape, making them an ideal comparison for flat objects or surfaces.

First Usage:

The phrase appeared in the English language as early as the 19th century, primarily used to describe geographic features or flat terrain.

Examples in Sentences:

"The road through the desert was as flat as a pancake."

"After the bike's tire went flat, it was literally as flat as a pancake."

"The joke fell flat during the presentation—it was as flat as a pancake."

Cultural Context:

The idiom "as flat as a pancake" is popular in English-speaking cultures, especially when describing landscapes like plains or deserts. It's also used metaphorically in everyday language to describe something dull, ineffective, or without variation.

Related Idioms in English:

"Flat as a board" – Another way to describe something extremely flat, often referring to surfaces.

"Fell flat" – Refers to something that failed to have the desired effect, such as a joke or idea.

Examples from Everyday Life:

Geography:

"The Midwest is known for being as flat as a pancake."

Objects:

"The basketball lost all its air and now it's as flat as a pancake."

Performance:

"His singing was off-key, and the performance was as flat as a pancake."

Conclusion:

"As flat as a pancake" is a versatile idiom that captures the idea of extreme flatness. Its roots in everyday culinary practices make it relatable, while its metaphorical usage adds color to descriptions of ineffective performances or dull situations.

Notes:

"Like Wine, It Gets Better with Age" – Something That Improves Over Time

Meaning of the Idiom:

"Like wine, it gets better with age" refers to something or someone that becomes better, more valuable, or more refined as time passes. The idiom highlights how experience, development, or maturation can enhance quality, worth, or character.

History and Origins:

Reference to Wine:

The phrase originates from the process of wine aging, during which its flavor deepens and quality improves. In Western culture, wine symbolizes luxury and sophistication, further reinforcing the positive connotation of the idiom.

Popularity:

The idiom gained prominence in the 20th century, particularly in contexts related to people, relationships, art, or objects that grow in value or appeal over time.

Examples in Sentences:

"His talent as a writer is like wine—it gets better with age."

"That classic movie is like wine; it gets better with age every time you watch it."

"Their friendship is like wine, growing stronger and deeper with every passing year."

Cultural Context:

This idiom is commonly used in English-speaking cultures to describe individuals who enhance their skills, wisdom, or character as they age. It can also apply to material objects like wine, art, or vintage cars, which become more cherished and valuable over time.

Related Idioms in English:

"A fine wine improves with time" – A variation of the same idiom, emphasizing elegance and value.

"Aged to perfection" – Often used to describe people or things that have reached an ideal state through the passage of time.

Examples from Everyday Life:

People:

"She's like wine; her wisdom and grace get better with age."

Art:

"That painting, created decades ago, is like wine—it gets better with age as its historical significance grows."

Relationships:

"Their marriage is like wine; it has only improved as they've grown together over the years."

Conclusion:

"Like wine, it gets better with age" is a timeless idiom celebrating the enriching effects of time. Whether referring to personal growth, enduring relationships, or treasured objects, it underscores the idea that some things truly improve and gain greater significance as they mature.

Notes:

"Half-Baked Idea" – An Incomplete or Poorly Thought-Out Idea

Meaning of the Idiom:

"Half-baked idea" refers to a concept, plan, or suggestion that is underdeveloped, poorly thought out, or not ready for implementation. The phrase implies that more time, effort, or detailed planning is needed before the idea can succeed.

History and Origins:

Culinary Roots:

The idiom originates from the process of baking, where "half-baked" means something that hasn't been cooked thoroughly, leaving it unfinished or subpar.

Spread of the Idiom:

The phrase gained popularity in the 19th and 20th centuries, particularly in contexts such as business, politics, and creative planning, where the importance of thorough preparation is emphasized.

Examples in Sentences:

"We can't present this half-baked idea to the client—it needs more work."

"Her plan to start a business without a budget was clearly a half-baked idea."

"Launching the product without proper testing is a half-baked idea that could backfire."

Cultural Context:

The idiom is commonly used in professional and personal settings to highlight the need for better preparation or deeper consideration. While it carries a mildly critical tone, it is often used humorously in informal situations.

Related Idioms in English:

"Put the cart before the horse" – To do things in the wrong order, often leading to problems.

"Jump the gun" – To act too quickly without adequate preparation.

Examples from Everyday Life:

Work:

"The presentation felt rushed and incomplete—it was a half-baked idea at best."

Business:

"Starting a company without a solid business plan is a half-baked idea."

Personal:

"His suggestion to move abroad without a job lined up was a half-baked idea."

Conclusion:

"Half-baked idea" is a vivid idiom that emphasizes the importance of thorough preparation and critical thinking. Its culinary origins make it relatable, while its application in various contexts highlights the universal need for careful planning and execution.

Notes:

"In Hot Water" – Being in Trouble

Meaning of the Idiom:

"In hot water" refers to being in a difficult or problematic situation, often due to a mistake or inappropriate behavior. It suggests a state where someone must face the consequences of their actions.

History and Origins:

Metaphor of Hot Water:

The idiom originates from the image of being in hot water, which is uncomfortable and potentially dangerous, symbolizing situations requiring immediate attention or resolution.

Early Usage:

The phrase was used as early as the 16th century in English literature, often to describe individuals who found themselves in trouble because of their decisions.

Examples in Sentences:

"He found himself in hot water after missing several deadlines at work."

"She's in hot water with her parents for staying out past curfew."

"The politician landed in hot water after his controversial comments."

Cultural Context:

The idiom "in hot water" is widely used in English-speaking cultures in both formal and informal settings. It is commonly employed to describe troubles arising from various scenarios, including workplace issues, family conflicts, legal troubles, or social controversies.

Related Idioms in English:

"In a pickle" – To be in a difficult or awkward situation.

"In deep trouble" – To be in serious problems or difficulties.

Examples from Everyday Life:

Work:

"He's in hot water with his boss for arriving late to an important meeting."

Family:

"The kids are in hot water for breaking the neighbor's window while playing."

Public Life:

"The celebrity found herself in hot water after her controversial social media post."

Conclusion:

"In hot water" is a versatile idiom that effectively conveys the urgency and discomfort of being in trouble. Its origins in vivid imagery make it relatable, and its wide applicability ensures it remains a staple in both formal and casual conversations.

Notes:

5. Idioms About Food and Emotions

"Bite Off More Than You Can Chew" – Taking on Too Much

Meaning of the Idiom:

"Bite off more than you can chew" refers to taking on tasks or responsibilities that exceed one's abilities or resources. The idiom is often used as a warning against overestimating one's capacity or committing to more than one can handle.

History and Origins:

Literal Meaning:

The phrase stems from a metaphor about eating, where someone takes too large a bite and struggles to chew or swallow it.

First Usage:

The idiom gained popularity in the United States during the 19th century, particularly as advice against overly ambitious undertakings.

Evolution of the Meaning:

Over time, the phrase extended beyond eating and came to describe challenges in work, personal life, and daily responsibilities.

Examples in Sentences:

"I think I've bitten off more than I can chew by agreeing to organize both events this week."

"He bit off more than he could chew when he promised to finish the project in just two days."

"Starting a new business while studying full-time might be biting off more than you can chew."

Cultural Context:

This idiom is widely used in English-speaking cultures, particularly when discussing personal or professional challenges. It has a mildly cautionary tone, encouraging realistic self-assessment and resource management.

Related Idioms in English:

"Spread oneself too thin" – Taking on too many tasks at once, leading to a drop in performance quality.

"Overreach" – Attempting to achieve something beyond one's capabilities.

Examples from Everyday Life:

Work:

"Taking on two major clients at once might mean biting off more than you can chew."

Family:

"She bit off more than she could chew by volunteering to host both Thanksgiving and Christmas dinners."

Personal Projects:

"I realized I'd bitten off more than I could chew when I decided to remodel the house by myself."

Conclusion:

"Bite off more than you can chew" is a relatable idiom that emphasizes the importance of knowing one's limits and being realistic about commitments. Its roots in a simple, everyday action—eating—make it an accessible and universally understood expression, applicable to a wide range of situations.

"Bread and Butter" – The Essentials for Living

Meaning of the Idiom:

"Bread and butter" refers to the basic means of living or one's primary source of income. It is often used to describe a job or activity that provides financial stability or essential elements required for everyday life.

History and Origins:

Culinary Roots:

Bread and butter have been staple components of diets in many cultures for centuries, symbolizing simplicity and necessity.

Early Usage:

The phrase "bread and butter" appeared in English as early as the 18th century, initially referring to essential sustenance for survival.

Evolution of the Metaphor:

Over time, the idiom extended beyond literal sustenance to describe key sources of income or fundamental aspects of a given field.

Examples in Sentences:

"Teaching is her bread and butter—it's how she supports her family."

"For many small towns, tourism is their bread and butter."

"The software company's bread and butter is their flagship product."

Cultural Context:

The idiom "bread and butter" is widely used in English-speaking cultures, appearing in both casual and formal conversations. It underscores the importance of fundamental components for economic or functional stability, often associated with livelihood or the core of an enterprise.

Related Idioms in English:

"Make ends meet" – To ensure one has enough resources to survive.

"Means of livelihood" – Refers to income or work that provides the basics for living.

Examples from Everyday Life:

Work:

"Freelancing may be fun, but my bread and butter comes from my full-time job."

Economy:

"Agriculture has always been the bread and butter of this region."

Business:

"Customer service is their bread and butter—it's what sets them apart from competitors."

Conclusion:

"Bread and butter" is a universally relatable idiom that highlights the essential aspects of life, whether referring to personal income, an economic foundation, or key components of success. Its roots in basic sustenance make it a timeless metaphor for necessity and stability.

Notes:

"Take with a Grain of Salt" – Approach with Skepticism

Meaning of the Idiom:

<u>"Take with a grain of salt"</u> means to approach something with caution or skepticism. It suggests that one should not fully trust or accept information, opinions, or promises without additional verification or context, as they may be exaggerated, incomplete, or unreliable.

History and Origins:

Ancient Roots:

The idiom originates from the Latin phrase <u>"cum grano salis"</u> (with a grain of salt), recorded by the Roman author Pliny the Elder in "Natural History." It referred to a recipe for neutralizing poison using a pinch of salt, metaphorically implying a cautious or measured approach to situations.

Development in English:

The expression was adopted into English in the 17th century, gaining its current meaning of skepticism toward information.

Examples in Sentences:

"I'd take his promises with a grain of salt—he often exaggerates."

"The article sounds convincing, but you should take it with a grain of salt until you verify the facts."

"She always tells dramatic stories, so I take her complaints with a grain of salt."

Cultural Context:

The idiom <u>"take with a grain of salt"</u> is widely used in English-speaking cultures, particularly when discussing rumors, public opinions, or unverified information. It emphasizes the importance of critical thinking and not taking everything at face value.

Related Idioms in English:

"Don't believe everything you hear" – A caution against blindly trusting information.

"Read between the lines" – To interpret something deeper, considering hidden or unspoken implications.

Examples from Everyday Life:

Media:

"I take everything I see on social media with a grain of salt—not everything is true."

Work:

"When he brags about his achievements, I take it with a grain of salt."

Relationships:

"Her account of the argument was very one-sided, so I took it with a grain of salt."

Conclusion:

"Take with a grain of salt" is a practical idiom that encourages skepticism and critical thinking. Its ancient origins and continued relevance highlight the timeless need for caution when interpreting information, whether in personal relationships, professional environments, or media consumption.

Notes:

"Food for Thought" – Something That Stimulates Thinking

Meaning of the Idiom:

"Food for thought" refers to ideas, concepts, or information that encourage reflection or deeper contemplation. It describes something that inspires analysis or sparks meaningful discussion.

History and Origins:

Culinary Reference:

The idiom uses the metaphor of food as sustenance for the body, likening it to thoughts as nourishment for the mind.

Early Usage:

The phrase first appeared in the 17th century in literary and philosophical contexts, emphasizing the importance of profound thinking.

Evolution:

Over time, the idiom became widely adopted in everyday language, particularly in education, literature, and media.

Examples in Sentences:

"The professor's lecture on climate change gave us a lot of food for thought."

"Her comments during the debate provided food for thought about the future of education."

"The book isn't an easy read, but it's definitely food for thought."

Cultural Context:

"Food for thought" is commonly used in English-speaking cultures in academic, philosophical, and professional contexts. It is valued for its ability to express the importance of engaging with ideas that inspire intellectual or personal growth.

Related Idioms in English:

"Something to think about" – Refers to an idea worth considering.

"Worth pondering" – Indicates something deserving of deeper reflection.

Examples from Everyday Life:

Education:

"The teacher's question about ethics in technology was real food for thought for the students."

Work:

"The CEO's vision for the company's future gave the board members food for thought."

Personal Growth:

"Her advice about work-life balance was definitely food for thought."

Conclusion:

"Food for thought" is a versatile idiom that highlights the intellectual and personal nourishment derived from thought-provoking ideas. Its metaphorical connection to sustenance makes it a relatable and universally appreciated expression, encouraging reflection in diverse contexts.

"Butter Someone Up" – To Flatter Someone

Meaning of the Idiom:

"Butter someone up" means to excessively compliment or flatter someone, usually with the intention of gaining a favor or achieving a personal goal. The phrase often implies insincerity or manipulation.

History and Origins:

Culinary Reference:

The idiom draws on the metaphor of spreading butter to make something smooth and appealing. Similarly, flattering someone is seen as a way to "soften" them to gain their favor.

Early Usage:

The phrase has roots in Indian traditions where offering butter to the gods symbolized devotion and a request for blessings. It entered English usage in the 19th century, taking on a figurative meaning.

Examples in Sentences:

"He tried to butter up his boss by complimenting her leadership skills."

"Don't try to butter me up—I'm not changing my decision."

"She's always buttering up her teachers to get better grades."

Cultural Context:

The idiom "butter someone up" is widely used in English-speaking cultures in both formal and informal settings. It is often associated with workplace dynamics, academic environments, or social relationships where flattery is used strategically.

Related Idioms in English:

"Kiss up to someone" – To overly praise or flatter someone to gain their approval.

"Flatter to deceive" – To use compliments as a means to mislead or manipulate someone.

Examples from Everyday Life:

Work:

"He's buttering up the manager because he wants a promotion."

School:

"She buttered up her professor with compliments before asking for an extension on her paper."

Family:

"The kids tried to butter up their mom by doing the dishes before asking for extra screen time."

Conclusion:

"Butter someone up" is a colorful idiom that captures the subtle art of using flattery to achieve one's goals. Its culinary origins make it easy to visualize, while its widespread use highlights its relevance in various personal and professional contexts.

Notes:

"Spill the Beans" – Reveal a Secret

Meaning of the Idiom:

"Spill the beans" means to disclose a secret or confidential information that was meant to remain private. It is often used to describe either an accidental or intentional act of revealing sensitive details.

History and Origins:

Ancient Roots:

The phrase is believed to have originated from the practice of voting in ancient Greece, where beans were used as a tool for secret ballots. Spilling the beans symbolized accidentally revealing the results before the vote count was complete.

Adoption in English:

The idiom entered the English language in the early 20th century and quickly became a popular expression for disclosing secrets.

Examples in Sentences:

"Don't spill the beans about the surprise party—it's supposed to be a secret!"

"She accidentally spilled the beans about the company's new product launch."

"If you know the answer, don't spill the beans—let everyone figure it out."

Cultural Context:

The idiom "spill the beans" is widely used in casual conversations and popular culture, especially when discussing situations involving secrets or surprises. It can be applied in both lighthearted and serious contexts.

Related Idioms in English:

"Let the cat out of the bag" – To reveal a secret or surprise.

"Blow the whistle" – To expose something illegal or unethical that was meant to be hidden.

Examples from Everyday Life:

Friends:

"He spilled the beans about their engagement before they could announce it themselves."

Work:

"The intern spilled the beans about the upcoming merger during lunch."

Family:

"Grandpa almost spilled the beans about the Christmas gifts!"

Conclusion:

"Spill the beans" is a colorful idiom that vividly conveys the act of revealing secrets. Its origins in ancient Greek voting practices give it a historical depth, while its widespread use today ensures its relevance in both casual and professional settings.

Notes:

"Eat Humble Pie" – Accept Defeat or Mistake with Humility

Meaning of the Idiom:

"Eat humble pie" means to admit a mistake or accept defeat in a humble and apologetic manner. The phrase suggests the need to accept embarrassment or take responsibility for wrongful actions.

History and Origins:

Culinary Roots:

The idiom originates from medieval England, where "umbles" referred to the internal organs of animals (e.g., heart, liver). These were often baked into pies and served to lower-class individuals, symbolizing humility. Eating such a pie reflected modesty and acceptance of one's lower status.

Evolution of Meaning:

Over time, the phrase took on a metaphorical meaning, referring to acknowledging one's errors or shortcomings.

Examples in Sentences:

"After blaming his team for the failure, he had to eat humble pie when it turned out he made the mistake."

"The politician was forced to eat humble pie after his controversial statement was proven wrong."

"She had to eat humble pie and apologize when she realized she was in the wrong."

Cultural Context:

"Eat humble pie" is widely used in professional, political, and personal contexts, often when someone needs to admit they were wrong or accept the consequences of their actions. It emphasizes the importance of humility and accountability.

Related Idioms in English:

"Swallow your pride" – To set aside one's ego and admit fault or accept help.

"Face the music" – To confront the consequences of one's actions.

Examples from Everyday Life:

Work:

"The manager had to eat humble pie and admit that the employees' suggestions improved the project."

Family:

"After arguing with her brother, she ate humble pie and apologized for being too harsh."

Public Life:

"The celebrity ate humble pie after the public backlash to her insensitive comments."

Conclusion:

"Eat humble pie" is a powerful idiom that encapsulates the act of acknowledging mistakes or misjudgments with humility. Its historical roots in medieval cuisine add depth to its metaphorical meaning, making it a timeless expression of the human need for accountability.

Notes:

6. Animals in food idioms

"Beef Up" – Strengthen or Improve Something

Meaning of the Idiom:

"Beef up" means to enhance, strengthen, or improve something to make it more effective, efficient, or impressive. It is commonly used in contexts involving plans, systems, structures, or even physical conditioning.

History and Origins:

Reference to Beef (Meat):

The phrase derives from the notion of "adding muscle" or "increasing bulk," which metaphorically refers to making something stronger or more substantial.

Adoption in English:

The idiom gained popularity in the 20th century, particularly in contexts like military, business, and technology, emphasizing the need to enhance resources or systems.

Examples in Sentences:

"We need to beef up our security system to prevent further breaches."

"He decided to beef up his resume by taking additional courses."

"The team beefed up their offense for the upcoming match."

Cultural Context:

The idiom "beef up" is widely used in English-speaking cultures in both formal and informal settings. It can refer to physical strengthening, as in fitness, or metaphorical improvements, such as upgrading technology, bolstering defenses, or enhancing capabilities.

Related Idioms in English:

"Fortify" – To strengthen something, especially in a defensive context.

"Bulk up" – To increase mass or strength, often used in fitness contexts.

Examples from Everyday Life:

Work:

"The company plans to beef up its IT department to handle increased workloads."

Personal Development:

"She beefed up her portfolio by adding more diverse projects."

Sports:

"The coach told the players to beef up their defense before the next game."

Conclusion:

"Beef up" is a versatile idiom that vividly conveys the concept of strengthening or improving something, whether it's a system, skill, or physical capacity. Its metaphorical roots in adding muscle make it a relatable and widely applicable expression in various contexts.

Notes:

"Chicken Out" – To Get Scared and Back Out

Meaning of the Idiom:

"Chicken out" means to lose courage and withdraw from a situation, especially one that requires bravery or confidence. The phrase is often used to describe instances where someone decides against taking a risk due to fear.

History and Origins:

Behavior of Chickens:

The idiom originates from the perception of chickens as timid and easily frightened animals, symbolizing cowardice or fear.

Adoption in English:

The phrase gained popularity in the 20th century, particularly in the United States, and is now commonly used in informal conversations to highlight cowardly behavior.

Examples in Sentences:

"He wanted to try skydiving but chickened out at the last minute."

"She chickened out of asking her boss for a raise."

"Don't chicken out now – we've come this far!"

Cultural Context:

"Chicken out" is widely used in casual, informal settings, often among younger generations. It frequently appears in conversations about challenges, competitions, or social situations where bravery or confidence is put to the test.

Related Idioms in English:

"Lose your nerve" – To lose courage at the critical moment.

"Back out" – To withdraw from something one previously committed to.

Examples from Everyday Life:

Adventure:

"He was ready to bungee jump but chickened out when he saw how high it was."

Work:

"She was about to present her idea in the meeting but chickened out at the last second."

Social Life:

"They planned to confess their feelings but chickened out when the moment came."

Conclusion:

"Chicken out" is a vivid and relatable idiom that conveys the idea of backing out due to fear. Its roots in the behavior of chickens make it an accessible metaphor, and its informal tone ensures its relevance in everyday conversations about courage and hesitation.

Notes:

"Pig Out" – To Overeat or Indulge in Excessive Eating

Meaning of the Idiom:

"Pig out" refers to eating excessively, often in an uncontrolled or greedy manner. The idiom is commonly used in informal settings to describe situations where someone overeats, especially during parties or while enjoying favorite foods.

History and Origins:

Behavior of Pigs:

The phrase originates from the observation of pigs, which are known for eating quickly and greedily. In English, the term "pig" has often been associated with overindulgence or lack of restraint.

Adoption in English:

The idiom "pig out" became popular in the 20th century, particularly in American slang, as a humorous way to describe excessive eating.

Examples in Sentences:

"We pigged out on pizza and ice cream at the party last night."

"Every Thanksgiving, he pigs out on turkey and stuffing."

"I told myself I'd eat healthy, but I ended up pigging out on snacks while watching TV."

Cultural Context:

The idiom "pig out" is used informally, often in a lighthearted or humorous tone. It is frequently employed to describe indulgent eating at social gatherings, holiday feasts, or casual moments of self-indulgence.

Related Idioms in English:

"Stuff oneself" – To eat a large amount of food, often to the point of discomfort.

"Eat like a horse" – To consume a lot of food.

Examples from Everyday Life:

Social Gatherings:

"At the buffet, everyone pigged out on the delicious desserts."

Holidays:

"I always pig out during Christmas – it's hard to resist all the treats."

Casual Moments:

"They pigged out on burgers and fries after the game."

Conclusion:

"Pig out" is a colorful and humorous idiom that captures the idea of overeating with a playful edge. Its roots in the behavior of pigs make it a vivid metaphor, and its informal tone ensures its place in casual conversations about food and indulgence.

Notes:

"Go Cold Turkey" – To Quit Something Abruptly

Meaning of the Idiom:

"Go cold turkey" means to suddenly and completely stop doing something, especially an addictive habit, without any gradual reduction. The idiom is commonly used in the context of quitting smoking, drinking, or other dependencies.

History and Origins:

Literal Reference:

One theory suggests the phrase comes from the physical symptoms experienced during withdrawal, such as chills and pale skin, which resemble the appearance of raw turkey (cold turkey).

Popularity:

The idiom became widely used in the 20th century, particularly in the United States, to describe abrupt cessation of addictive behaviors.

Examples in Sentences:

"After years of smoking, he decided to go cold turkey and hasn't touched a cigarette since."

"She went cold turkey on sugar and started a healthier lifestyle."

"It's hard to go cold turkey on caffeine, but sometimes it's necessary."

Cultural Context:

The phrase "go cold turkey" is frequently used in conversations about health, lifestyle changes, and addiction recovery. It emphasizes the challenge and determination required to quit something abruptly, often evoking sympathy or admiration.

Related Idioms in English:

"Kick the habit" – To quit an addiction or bad habit.

"Quit cold" – To stop doing something suddenly and completely.

Examples from Everyday Life:

Health:

"He went cold turkey on junk food after his doctor warned him about his cholesterol levels."

Addictions:

"She decided to go cold turkey and stop drinking energy drinks altogether."

Work:

"I went cold turkey on checking my email during weekends to improve my work-life balance."

Conclusion:

"Go cold turkey" is a powerful idiom that encapsulates the difficulty and determination involved in quitting something suddenly. Its vivid metaphor, drawn from withdrawal symptoms, makes it a relatable and impactful expression in discussions about personal transformation and overcoming challenges.

Notes:

"Like a Fish Out of Water" – To Feel Out of Place

Meaning of the Idiom:

"Like a fish out of water" describes a feeling of discomfort, awkwardness, or being unfit for a new environment, situation, or group. It conveys a sense of not belonging or struggling to adapt.

History and Origins:

Literal Reference:

The phrase stems from the observation that fish cannot function properly outside their natural habitat, water.

First Usage:

The idiom dates back to medieval times and has been a part of English literature since the 14th century. It was initially used as a metaphor to depict situations where someone feels uneasy or misplaced.

Examples in Sentences:

"When he started his new job in a foreign country, he felt like a fish out of water."

"She was like a fish out of water at the formal event – she's more comfortable in casual settings."

"As the only beginner in the advanced class, I felt like a fish out of water."

Cultural Context:

The idiom "like a fish out of water" is widely used in English-speaking cultures, in both informal and formal conversations. It applies to various aspects of life, such as adapting to new workplaces, navigating social circles, or entering unfamiliar environments.

Related Idioms in English:

"Out of your element" – Being in a situation where one feels uncomfortable or unprepared.

"A square peg in a round hole" – Someone who doesn't fit into a specific environment or role.

Examples from Everyday Life:

Work:

"He felt like a fish out of water during his first day at the new job."

Travel:

"I don't speak the language, so I feel like a fish out of water here."

Social Situations:

"At the fancy dinner party, she was like a fish out of water in her casual jeans."

Conclusion:

"Like a fish out of water" is a vivid metaphor that effectively conveys the discomfort of being in an unfamiliar or unsuitable setting. Its universal application makes it a relatable expression for a wide range of experiences.

"Kill the Goose That Lays the Golden Egg" – Destroying Something Valuable

Meaning of the Idiom:

"Kill the goose that lays the golden egg" refers to the act of destroying or sacrificing something valuable due to greed, impatience, or short-sightedness. The idiom warns against actions that result in the loss of a steady source of benefits or prosperity.

History and Origins:

Aesop's Fable:

The phrase originates from one of Aesop's fables, where a farmer owned a goose that laid golden eggs. Driven by greed, he killed the goose hoping to find more gold inside, only to lose his source of wealth entirely.

Evolution of Meaning:

Over time, the idiom became a metaphorical warning against impulsive decisions that jeopardize long-term gains for short-term rewards.

Examples in Sentences:

"By overworking their employees, the company risks killing the goose that lays the golden egg."

"Raising ticket prices too high might kill the goose that lays the golden egg by driving away loyal customers."

"He sold the profitable business for quick cash, killing the goose that laid the golden egg."

Cultural Context:

This idiom is frequently used in business, economics, and everyday conversations to caution against shortsighted decisions. It emphasizes the importance of nurturing valuable resources rather than exploiting them recklessly.

Related Idioms in English:

"Don't cut off your nose to spite your face" – Avoid actions that cause more harm than good.

"Bite the hand that feeds you" – Do not harm or alienate someone who provides support or benefits.

Examples from Daily Life:

Business:

"If they focus only on short-term profits, they might kill the goose that lays the golden egg."

Personal Finance:

"Withdrawing all the money from the trust fund is like killing the goose that lays the golden egg."

Relationships:

"Ignoring the needs of your most supportive friend is like killing the goose that lays the golden egg."

Conclusion:

The idiom "Kill the goose that lays the golden egg" serves as a timeless reminder of the dangers of greed and shortsightedness. It encourages preserving and valuing resources that provide sustained benefits rather than jeopardizing them for fleeting gains.

"Bring Home the Bacon" – Earning a Living

Meaning of the Idiom:

"Bring home the bacon" means earning money to support oneself and one's family. The phrase refers to work and providing for essential needs, often implying being the main income earner in a household.

History and Origins:

Early References:

The idiom dates back to 12th-century England, where some villages rewarded married couples who demonstrated exceptional harmony with bacon as a symbol of their success.

Modern Usage:

The phrase gained its current meaning in the 20th century, particularly in the United States. Bacon, representing food as a basic necessity, metaphorically illustrates bringing income home to sustain life.

Examples in Sentences:

"He works two jobs to bring home the bacon for his family."

"As the sole breadwinner, she brings home the bacon to support her kids."

"They rely on him to bring home the bacon, especially during tough times."

Cultural Context:

"Bring home the bacon" is widely used in English-speaking cultures, especially in conversations about work, economics, and family responsibilities. It often highlights hard work and dedication to supporting loved ones financially.

Related Idioms in English:

"Earn a living" – Making money to cover basic needs.

"Make ends meet" – Earning just enough to manage financial obligations.

Examples from Daily Life:

Work:

"She's been working overtime to bring home the bacon and save for a new house."

Family:

"As a stay-at-home dad, he takes care of the kids while she brings home the bacon."

Career:

"He chose a stable job in finance to reliably bring home the bacon."

Conclusion:

The idiom "Bring home the bacon" captures the essence of providing for one's household through hard work and determination. It reflects the importance of financial stability and the effort required to ensure that basic needs are met.

Notes:

Eat Like a Bird" – To Eat Very Little

Meaning of the Idiom:

"Eat like a bird" refers to consuming very small portions of food, often in a delicate or picky manner. The phrase describes people who eat less than an average meal size.

History and Origins:

Literal Reference:

The idiom originates from the observation of birds, which appear to eat small amounts due to their size. However, in reality, some birds consume a significant amount relative to their body weight.

Spread of Usage:

The expression gained popularity in the 19th and 20th centuries, especially in casual English, to humorously or critically comment on eating habits.

Examples in Sentences:

"She eats like a bird – one small salad is enough to fill her up."

"He's always been thin because he eats like a bird at every meal."

"Don't worry about cooking too much for her – she eats like a bird."

Cultural Context:

The idiom "eat like a bird" is commonly used in informal conversations, often to humorously describe someone's eating habits. It can carry a playful tone or sometimes a slight critique when discussing small appetites or picky eaters.

Related Idioms in English:

"Nibble at something" – To eat in small amounts, like snacking or grazing.

"Pick at your food" – To eat minimally, often out of lack of appetite or interest.

Examples from Daily Life:

Dining out:

"We ordered a lot of food, but she ate like a bird and barely touched her plate."

Family:

"My mom always says I eat like a bird because I never finish my meals."

Friends:

"He eats like a bird, so there's always plenty of leftovers when we order together."

Conclusion:

The idiom "eat like a bird" captures the essence of small or delicate eating habits. Whether used to describe someone with a tiny appetite or a preference for light eating, the phrase remains a humorous and relatable way to discuss food behaviors.

Notes:

"Squeeze Blood from a Turnip" – Demanding the Impossible

Meaning of the Idiom:

"Squeeze blood from a turnip" refers to attempting to achieve something that is impossible, particularly when making unrealistic demands or expecting results from an inadequate source. It is often used in contexts where someone is trying to extract money, effort, or resources from a person or situation that simply cannot deliver.

History and Origins:

Literal Reference:

The idiom stems from the image of a turnip, a vegetable incapable of producing blood, symbolizing the futility of attempting the impossible.

First Usage:

The phrase appeared in English literature during the 18th century, emphasizing the absurdity or irony of such efforts.

Regional Variations:

In some cultures, different vegetables or objects are substituted, maintaining the same metaphor of an unattainable goal.

Examples in Sentences:

"You can't get him to pay more – it's like trying to squeeze blood from a turnip."

"Expecting her to finish the project in one day is like squeezing blood from a turnip."

"They tried to negotiate better terms, but it was like squeezing blood from a turnip."

Cultural Context:

The idiom is commonly used in English-speaking cultures, especially in financial, negotiation, or work-related scenarios. It highlights the frustration or futility of trying to extract something impossible, often with a touch of humor or irony.

Related Idioms in English:

"Get water from a stone" – Attempting to achieve the unachievable.

"Barking up the wrong tree" – Pursuing something in an incorrect or fruitless manner.

Examples from Daily Life:

Work:

"The manager asked for higher productivity from an already overworked team – like squeezing blood from a turnip."

Finance:

"Trying to collect rent from a tenant who's bankrupt is like squeezing blood from a turnip."

Family:

"Asking my brother for emotional advice is like squeezing blood from a turnip – he's not the empathetic type."

Conclusion:

"Squeeze blood from a turnip" is a vivid idiom that encapsulates the frustration of demanding what cannot be delivered. Whether applied to financial struggles, workplace expectations, or personal relationships, it serves as a reminder of the importance of setting realistic goals and understanding limitations.

Notes:

"Cook Someone's Goose" – Ruin Someone's Plans

Meaning of the Idiom:

"Cook someone's goose" means to ruin someone's plans, hopes, or chances of success. It is often used in situations where deliberate actions result in someone's failure or inability to achieve their goals.

History and Origins:

Etymology:

The phrase has several theories about its origin, with the most popular linking it to the 18th century, where "cooking a goose" became a metaphor for actions leading to someone's downfall.

Alternative Legend:

A story suggests that during a Swedish invasion, townsfolk were preparing a festive goose, which the invaders mistook as a taunt. In retaliation, they destroyed the town, "cooking their goose" symbolically.

Modern Usage:

Over time, the idiom took on a figurative meaning, referring to situations where plans or ambitions are sabotaged.

Examples in Sentences:

"She cooked his goose by revealing his plans to the boss."

"The team's chance to win was cooked when their star player got injured."

"He thought he could cheat on the test, but the teacher caught him and cooked his goose."

Cultural Context:

"Cook someone's goose" is commonly used in informal conversations, especially to describe betrayal, disappointment, or unexpected actions that lead to failure. It often carries a humorous or ironic tone.

Related Idioms in English:

"Rain on someone's parade" – Spoil someone's fun or plans.

"Throw a wrench in the works" – Disrupt plans or cause problems.

Examples from Daily Life:

Work:

"He cooked his own goose by missing the deadline for the project."

Sports:

"The referee's controversial call cooked their goose in the final minutes of the game."

Relationships:

"When she lied about her plans, it really cooked her goose with her friends."

Conclusion:

"Cook someone's goose" vividly captures the frustration and consequences of having one's plans sabotaged. Whether it's due to external interference or one's own mistakes, the idiom highlights how quickly aspirations can crumble when circumstances take an unexpected turn.

Notes:

7. Culinary Idioms Related to Time and Action

"In a Nutshell" – In Brief

Meaning of the Idiom:

"In a nutshell" means to present something in a very concise and straightforward manner. It is used when someone wants to convey the essence of a matter without delving into unnecessary details.

History and Origins:

Literal Reference:

The phrase originates from the idea of fitting something small, like the essence of a story or explanation, into the shell of a nut (nutshell).

Early Usage:

The idiom appeared in English literature in the 17th century. One notable reference is found in Shakespeare's Hamlet: "I could be bounded in a nutshell and count myself a king of infinite space."

Evolution of Meaning:

Over time, the phrase came to symbolize brevity and simplicity in communication.

Examples in Sentences:

"In a nutshell, we need more time to complete the project."

"She explained the plan in a nutshell: more funding, better results."

"In a nutshell, their idea is to simplify the process and save money."

Cultural Context:

"In a nutshell" is widely used across English-speaking cultures in both formal and informal settings. The phrase is valued for its practicality, especially when delivering quick summaries or important information without elaboration.

Related Idioms in English:

"To make a long story short" – To summarize by leaving out unnecessary details.

"Get to the point" – To focus directly on the main topic or issue.

Examples from Daily Life:

Work:

"In a nutshell, the client wants a simpler design for the website."

Education:

"The teacher summarized the lecture in a nutshell: work hard and stay consistent."

Daily Life:

"In a nutshell, the movie was great, but the ending was disappointing."

Conclusion:

"In a nutshell" is a versatile and widely appreciated idiom that encapsulates the essence of clarity and brevity. Whether in casual conversations or professional settings, it serves as a powerful tool for summarizing ideas and cutting through unnecessary complexity.

Notes:

"Hot Potato" – A Controversial Topic

Meaning of the Idiom:

"Hot potato" refers to a controversial issue or topic that evokes strong emotions and is difficult to handle. The idiom often describes situations where individuals avoid taking a stance because the subject is too sensitive or risky.

History and Origins:

Literal Reference:

The idiom originates from the image of a hot potato that is too hot to hold and must be quickly passed on.

Early Usage:

The phrase began to appear in the 19th century in informal English, describing issues that were "too hot" or dangerous to handle.

Evolution of Meaning:

Over time, the idiom gained traction in political and media contexts, becoming a go-to phrase for describing contentious social or economic problems.

Examples in Sentences:

"The issue of climate change has become a political hot potato."

"No one wants to address the hot potato of tax reform during the election year."

"The scandal was a hot potato that the company tried to avoid discussing."

Cultural Context:

"Hot potato" is widely used in political, social, and professional contexts. It frequently appears in public discussions about topics that provoke strong opinions or require careful handling to avoid backlash or controversy.

Related Idioms in English:

"A thorny issue" – A difficult and problematic matter.

"Walking on eggshells" – Behaving cautiously in a delicate situation.

Examples from Daily Life:

Politics:

"The policy on immigration remains a hot potato for the government."

Workplace:

"The budget cuts are a hot potato that no one wants to discuss at the meeting."

Media:

"The controversial decision by the celebrity became a hot potato on social media."

Conclusion:

"Hot potato" is an idiom that encapsulates the challenges of navigating sensitive or divisive topics. Its vivid imagery conveys the urgency and discomfort associated with controversial issues, making it a powerful expression in conversations about complexity and conflict.

Notes:

"Put All Your Eggs in One Basket" – Risking Everything on a Single Option

Meaning of the Idiom:

"Put all your eggs in one basket" refers to risking everything by focusing solely on one option without any backup. The idiom warns that failure could result in total loss, making it a high-risk action.

History and Origin:

Literal Reference: The idiom stems from the image of carrying eggs in one basket—if the basket falls, all the eggs break.

Early Usage: The phrase appeared in English literature in the 17th century and was often used as a warning against making risky decisions.

Popularity in Finance: The idiom gained particular traction in the context of investments and risk management, where diversification is emphasized as a critical strategy.

Examples of Usage in English:

"Don't put all your eggs in one basket by investing everything in one stock."

"She put all her eggs in one basket by applying to only one university."

"Starting a business without a backup plan is like putting all your eggs in one basket."

Cultural Context:

"Put all your eggs in one basket" is widely used across various fields, including finance, business, education, and personal life. The idiom emphasizes the importance of careful planning and avoiding risk-heavy decisions, particularly those with significant consequences.

Related Idioms in English:

"Don't bet everything on one horse" – Avoid risking everything on one option.

"Spread your bets" – Diversify your risk across multiple options.

Everyday Examples:

Finance: "It's risky to put all your eggs in one basket by relying solely on cryptocurrency investments."

Education: "Applying to multiple schools ensures you're not putting all your eggs in one basket."

Career: "He quit his job to focus on a startup, putting all his eggs in one basket."

Conclusion:

The idiom <u>"Put all your eggs in one basket"</u> serves as a cautionary reminder to avoid placing all your resources, effort, or trust into a single option. It underscores the value of diversification and risk management in achieving success across various aspects of life.

Notes:

Put All Your Eggs in One Basket" – Risking Everything on a Single Option

Meaning of the Idiom:

"Put all your eggs in one basket" refers to risking everything by focusing solely on one option without any backup. The idiom warns that failure could result in total loss, making it a high-risk action.

History and Origin:

Literal Reference: The idiom stems from the image of carrying eggs in one basket—if the basket falls, all the eggs break.

Early Usage: The phrase appeared in English literature in the 17th century and was often used as a warning against making risky decisions.

Popularity in Finance: The idiom gained particular traction in the context of investments and risk management, where diversification is emphasized as a critical strategy.

Examples of Usage in English:

"Don't put all your eggs in one basket by investing everything in one stock."

"She put all her eggs in one basket by applying to only one university."

"Starting a business without a backup plan is like putting all your eggs in one basket."

Cultural Context:

"Put all your eggs in one basket" is widely used across various fields, including finance, business, education, and personal life. The idiom emphasizes the importance of careful planning and avoiding risk-heavy decisions, particularly those with significant consequences.

Related Idioms in English:

"Don't bet everything on one horse" – Avoid risking everything on one option.

"Spread your bets" – Diversify your risk across multiple options.

Everyday Examples:

Finance: "It's risky to put all your eggs in one basket by relying solely on cryptocurrency investments."

Education: "Applying to multiple schools ensures you're not putting all your eggs in one basket."

Career: "He quit his job to focus on a startup, putting all his eggs in one basket."

Conclusion:

The idiom "Put all your eggs in one basket" serves as a cautionary reminder to avoid placing all your resources, effort, or trust into a single option. It underscores the value of diversification and risk management in achieving success across various aspects of life.

Notes:

"Have Bigger Fish to Fry" – To Have More Important Things to Do

Meaning of the Idiom:

"Have bigger fish to fry" means having more pressing or important matters to attend to than the current task or issue. The idiom implies that the present situation is less significant compared to other priorities.

History and Origin:

Literal Reference: The phrase originates from cooking, where frying a bigger fish symbolizes handling something more valuable or significant than a smaller one.

Early Usage: The idiom first appeared in English literature in the 17th century, used to denote the prioritization of more critical tasks.

Evolution: Over time, it began to be applied in social, professional, and personal contexts to highlight the hierarchy of tasks or responsibilities.

Examples of Usage in English:

"I can't worry about the party decorations right now – I have bigger fish to fry."

"The manager decided not to address the minor mistake because she had bigger fish to fry with the upcoming presentation."

"He ignored the gossip because he had bigger fish to fry, like preparing for his final exams."

Cultural Context:

"Have bigger fish to fry" is commonly used in both formal and informal settings. It frequently appears in conversations about work, daily life, and time management, emphasizing the importance of focusing on more critical or impactful responsibilities.

Related Idioms in English:

"More important fish to fry" – An alternative version of the same idiom.

"Other irons in the fire" – Refers to having other, more significant matters in progress.

Everyday Examples:

Work: "The report can wait until tomorrow – I have bigger fish to fry with this client meeting."

Family: "I won't argue about the TV tonight; I have bigger fish to fry with planning the family trip."

Social Life: "She didn't respond to the drama because she had bigger fish to fry with her new business launch."

Conclusion:

The idiom "Have bigger fish to fry" serves as a reminder to prioritize tasks and focus on what truly matters. It is a versatile expression used to underline the importance of managing time and energy effectively in both personal and professional contexts.

Notes:

"Like Two Peas in a Pod" – Very Similar to Each Other

Meaning of the Idiom:

"Like two peas in a pod" describes two people who are very similar in appearance or character, or who share a close bond. The phrase often highlights individuals who understand each other perfectly or have much in common.

History and Origin:

Literal Reference: The idiom originates from the appearance of peas growing in pods. Peas in the same pod are identical, serving as a metaphor for similarity or closeness.

First Usage: The phrase entered the English language in the 17th century to describe people or things that are inseparable or strikingly alike.

Evolution of Meaning: Over time, it became widely used in contexts involving personal relationships, especially between friends, siblings, or partners.

Examples of Usage in English:

"The twins are like two peas in a pod – they look and act exactly alike."

"They've been best friends since childhood, like two peas in a pod."

"When it comes to their sense of humor, they're like two peas in a pod."

Cultural Context:

"Like two peas in a pod" is a commonly used idiom in English-speaking cultures, often appearing in conversations about relationships, friendships, or similarities between people. It has a warm and positive connotation, emphasizing closeness or harmony.

Related Idioms in English:

"Cut from the same cloth" – Very similar in character or values.

"Birds of a feather flock together" – People with similar traits or interests tend to associate with one another.

Everyday Examples:

Family: "The sisters are like two peas in a pod – they share everything and finish each other's sentences."

Friendship: "John and Mike are like two peas in a pod, always together and sharing the same hobbies."

Workplace: "Those two colleagues are like two peas in a pod – they work perfectly as a team."

Conclusion:

The idiom "Like two peas in a pod" is a charming way to describe deep connections or similarities between individuals. It reflects warmth, harmony, and an inseparable bond, making it a beloved phrase in English-speaking cultures.

Notes:

"Out to Lunch" – Being Mentally Absent

Meaning of the Idiom:

"Out to lunch" describes someone who is distracted, inattentive, or mentally absent. The phrase can be used both literally, when someone is actually away for lunch, and figuratively, to highlight a lack of focus or awareness of their surroundings.

History and Origin:

Literal Meaning: The phrase originally referred to someone who was physically away, eating lunch, and therefore temporarily unavailable.

Metaphorical Use: By the mid-20th century, the idiom began to be used figuratively, describing individuals who appeared mentally absent or disconnected from reality. It gained popularity in American culture.

Examples of Usage in English:

"He seemed out to lunch during the meeting and didn't contribute at all."

"She's acting like she's out to lunch – I've asked her the same question three times!"

"When it comes to technology, he's completely out to lunch."

Cultural Context:

"Out to lunch" is commonly used in informal settings, often with a humorous or mildly critical tone. It is frequently applied in conversations about work, school, or everyday interactions to describe someone who seems unfocused or out of touch with what's happening around them.

Related Idioms in English:

"Head in the clouds" – Being detached from reality or daydreaming.

"Not all there" – Describing someone as being mentally distracted or absent.

Everyday Examples:

Work: "During the presentation, he was totally out to lunch – he didn't even notice when I asked him a question."

School: "The student seemed out to lunch today; she couldn't focus on anything."

Social Situations: "He's been out to lunch since he started thinking about his vacation plans."

Conclusion:

The idiom "Out to lunch" is a lighthearted way to describe someone who is mentally distracted or disengaged. Its figurative use adds humor or mild critique to everyday conversations, making it a versatile and relatable expression in English-speaking cultures.

Notes:

"Cook Up a Storm" – To Prepare Something with Enthusiasm and Flair

Meaning of the Idiom:

"Cook up a storm" means preparing a large amount of food with great enthusiasm or creating something impressive and energetic. The phrase is often used in a positive context, emphasizing effort, passion, and scale in the activity.

History and Origin:

Literal Reference: The phrase combines the imagery of a "storm," symbolizing intensity and energy, with "cook up," which refers to preparing food.

Development of Meaning: Originating in the 20th century, the idiom gained popularity in English-speaking cultures, first in informal conversations about cooking and later extending to describe energetic and creative actions in general.

Examples of Usage in English:

"She cooked up a storm in the kitchen for the holiday dinner – there was enough food for everyone and more!"

"He loves to cook up a storm whenever friends come over for a barbecue."

"The marketing team cooked up a storm with their latest campaign – it was a huge success."

Cultural Context:

"Cook up a storm" is commonly used in informal contexts, particularly to describe enthusiastic cooking or intense preparation for events. It frequently appears in discussions about holidays, parties, or creative projects that require a significant amount of effort and passion.

Related Idioms in English:

"Pull out all the stops" – To give your maximum effort or act with grandeur.

"Go all out" – To act with total commitment and enthusiasm.

Everyday Examples:

Cooking: "She cooked up a storm for her son's birthday party – the table was overflowing with dishes!"

Work: "The event planners cooked up a storm to make the conference unforgettable."

Social Life: "Whenever they host a dinner party, they cook up a storm and impress all their guests."

Conclusion:

The idiom "Cook up a storm" vividly captures the energy and enthusiasm of preparing something on a grand scale. Whether used literally for cooking or metaphorically for creative endeavors, it conveys a sense of dedication and impressive results.

Notes:

"Salt of the Earth" – A Very Good, Honest Person

Meaning of the Idiom:

"Salt of the earth" refers to a person who is exceptionally honest, kind, sincere, and trustworthy. The expression is often used as a compliment to describe someone who is humble, helpful, and embodies the best human qualities.

History and Origin:

Biblical Roots: The phrase originates from the Bible, specifically from Matthew 5:13, where Jesus says to his disciples, "You are the salt of the earth." In ancient times, salt was highly valued for its preservative and purifying qualities, symbolizing permanence, purity, and worth.

Evolution in English: Over time, the idiom came to be used metaphorically in English to describe people who are morally upright and form the solid foundation of society.

Examples of Usage in English:

"My grandmother was the salt of the earth – always kind and ready to help anyone in need."

"The volunteers who dedicate their time to helping the homeless are truly the salt of the earth."

"He may not be wealthy, but he's the salt of the earth, always there for his friends and family."

Cultural Context:

"Salt of the earth" is widely used in English-speaking cultures as an expression of respect and admiration for individuals who stand out for their humility and goodness. The phrase is often applied in contexts involving daily life, philanthropy, and interpersonal relationships.

Related Idioms in English:

"Heart of gold" – A person with a very kind and generous nature.

"Down to earth" – Someone who is humble and practical.

Everyday Examples:

Community: "The local farmer, known for his generosity and honesty, is the salt of the earth."

Family: "My uncle is the salt of the earth – he's always helping out his neighbors without expecting anything in return."

Workplace: "She's the salt of the earth in the office, always willing to lend a hand when someone's in trouble."

Conclusion:

The idiom "salt of the earth" highlights the profound value of kindness, integrity, and humility in human character. It serves as a timeless tribute to individuals who positively impact their communities and relationships through their genuine and selfless actions.

Notes:

"As Cool as a Cucumber" – Very Calm

Meaning of the Idiom:

"As cool as a cucumber" means being exceptionally calm, composed, and unflustered, especially in stressful or challenging situations. The expression highlights the ability to maintain a level head and logical thinking under pressure.

History and Origin:

Literal Reference: The phrase derives from the physical property of cucumbers, which remain cool to the touch even on hot days due to their high water content.

First Usage: The idiom appeared in English literature in the 18th century and quickly gained popularity as a metaphor for calmness and composure.

Spread of Usage: The phrase is commonly used in informal conversations, as well as in literature and media.

Examples of Usage in English:

"Even during the crisis, she remained as cool as a cucumber and handled the situation perfectly."

"He was as cool as a cucumber when he presented his idea to the board of directors."

"Despite the chaos around him, the pilot stayed as cool as a cucumber and landed the plane safely."

Cultural Context:

"As cool as a cucumber" is a widely recognized idiom in English-speaking cultures, often appearing in discussions about handling stress, pressure, or difficult circumstances. The expression carries a positive connotation, celebrating the ability to stay calm and composed.

Related Idioms in English:

"Keep your cool" – Maintain composure.

"Stay calm under pressure" – Remain calm in stressful situations.

Everyday Examples:

Work: "The manager was as cool as a cucumber during the heated meeting with the clients."

Social Life: "She's always as cool as a cucumber, even during big family gatherings."

Sports: "The goalkeeper was as cool as a cucumber during the penalty shootout."

Conclusion:

The idiom "as cool as a cucumber" is a testament to the value of staying composed and collected in difficult situations. It serves as a compliment to those who exhibit remarkable self-control and grace under pressure.

Notes:

"The Pot Calling the Kettle Black" – Hypocrisy

Meaning of the Idiom:

"The pot calling the kettle black" refers to someone accusing another of a fault or behavior they themselves exhibit. The idiom highlights hypocrisy, where criticism is ironic because the accuser shares the same flaw.

History and Origin:

Literal Reference: The phrase originates from the time when pots and kettles were made of cast iron and used over open fires, causing both to become blackened with soot. The irony lies in one blackened object criticizing another for the same condition.

First Usage: The idiom appeared in literature in the 17th century, including works like Cervantes' Don Quixote, where it was used to point out hypocrisy.

Development of Meaning: Over time, the idiom evolved into a metaphor for ironic accusations, used broadly to criticize those guilty of double standards.

Examples of Usage in English:

"It's the pot calling the kettle black when he complains about her being late – he's always late himself."

"She criticized him for being disorganized, but that's the pot calling the kettle black."

"The politician accusing others of corruption is a case of the pot calling the kettle black."

Cultural Context:

"The pot calling the kettle black" is widely used in English-speaking cultures, particularly in discussions about social behaviors, conflicts, and hypocrisy. It frequently appears in politics, workplace disputes, and interpersonal relationships to underline the irony of mutual accusations.

Related Idioms in English:

"People who live in glass houses shouldn't throw stones" – Criticizing others while being equally at fault.

"Hypocrisy knows no bounds" – Highlighting unlimited hypocrisy.

Everyday Examples:

Work: "When the messy colleague criticized my desk, it was the pot calling the kettle black."

Family: "My brother tells me to stop using my phone, but that's the pot calling the kettle black – he's always on his phone."

Politics: "The two candidates accusing each other of dishonesty is just the pot calling the kettle black."

Conclusion:

"The pot calling the kettle black" effectively captures the essence of hypocrisy, serving as a sharp reminder to examine one's own flaws before pointing out those of others. It's a timeless idiom that continues to find relevance in everyday conversations and societal critiques.

Notes:

8. Funny and Unusual Culinary Idioms

"Butterfingers" – Someone Who Drops Everything

Meaning of the Idiom:

"Butterfingers" refers to a clumsy person who frequently drops things or struggles to hold onto them. The term is often used humorously to describe mishaps, particularly when someone unintentionally lets something slip from their grasp.

History and Origin:

Literal Reference: The idiom stems from the idea that hands covered in butter (butterfingers) would be slippery, making it difficult to grip objects.

First Use: The phrase began appearing in 19th-century Britain and later gained popularity in the United States. It was featured in literature and advertisements, such as Butterfinger candy bar commercials in the 1920s.

Spread of Usage: The idiom quickly became a common term in sports, particularly football and baseball, to describe players who had trouble holding onto the ball.

Examples of Usage in English:

"I can't believe I dropped the vase – I'm such a butterfingers today!"

"The goalkeeper was called butterfingers after missing an easy catch."

"She's a bit of a butterfingers in the kitchen, always dropping utensils and glasses."

Cultural Context:

"Butterfingers" is widely used in everyday conversations, especially in humorous situations, to gently tease someone about their clumsiness. The idiom is also frequently applied in sports and pop culture to highlight moments of mishandling or lack of coordination.

Related Idioms in English:

"All thumbs" – Being clumsy, particularly with hands.

"Clumsy as an elephant" – Being very uncoordinated or awkward.

Examples from Daily Life:

Sports: "The player fumbled the ball and was called butterfingers by the fans."

Kitchen: "I can't trust him with the plates – he's a total butterfingers."

Daily Life: "Oops! I dropped my keys again – butterfingers strikes!"

Conclusion:

"Butterfingers" is a lighthearted idiom that turns moments of clumsiness into opportunities for humor. Its widespread usage across casual conversations, sports commentary, and pop culture makes it a relatable and amusing expression.

Notes:

"Full of Beans" – Full of Energy

Meaning of the Idiom:

"Full of beans" refers to being full of energy, enthusiasm, and vigor. It describes someone who is lively, cheerful, and ready to take on activities. Occasionally, the idiom can be used humorously or ironically to describe someone who is overly excited or hard to manage.

History and Origin:

Literal Reference: The phrase might stem from a diet rich in beans, traditionally considered an energy-boosting food.

First Usage: The idiom appeared in the 19th century in Britain, initially used to describe spirited horses that were fed beans to increase their energy.

Wider Usage: Over time, the idiom came to refer to people who are energetic and enthusiastic.

Examples of Usage in English:

"The kids were full of beans after the birthday party."

"He's always full of beans in the morning, ready to take on the day."

"You seem full of beans today – did something good happen?"

Cultural Context:

"Full of beans" is commonly used in informal conversations, especially when describing children, pets, or individuals who are very active and lively. The phrase has a positive tone, though it can occasionally imply mild annoyance if someone's energy is excessive.

Related Idioms in English:

"Bursting with energy" – Overflowing with vitality.

"Bright-eyed and bushy-tailed" – Enthusiastic and eager to act.

Examples from Daily Life:

Children: "After a good night's sleep, the kids woke up full of beans and ready to play."

Work: "Our new colleague is full of beans – he's already suggested several great ideas."

Social Life: "She arrived at the party full of beans, bringing joy and energy to everyone."

Conclusion:

"Full of beans" is a cheerful idiom that highlights liveliness and enthusiasm. Whether describing someone's natural energy or a temporary burst of excitement, the expression adds a playful and positive tone to conversations.

Notes:

"Couch Potato" – A Lazy Person Who Just Watches TV

Meaning of the Idiom:

"Couch potato" refers to a lazy person who spends most of their time lying or sitting on a couch, typically watching TV or engaging in other passive activities. The phrase is often used humorously, though it can carry a mildly negative connotation.

History and Origin:

Literal Reference: The term combines the image of a person lounging on a couch with a potato, symbolizing inactivity and passivity.

First Usage: The idiom was popularized in the 1970s in the United States when a comedy group used it to humorously describe people addicted to watching TV.

Wider Adoption: The phrase quickly entered common language thanks to its comedic appeal and references in popular culture.

Examples of Usage in English:

"He spent the entire weekend as a couch potato, binge-watching his favorite TV series."

"Don't be such a couch potato – let's go for a walk!"

"She used to be a couch potato, but now she exercises regularly."

Cultural Context:

"Couch potato" is a widely recognized idiom in English-speaking cultures, often used in light-hearted conversations about lazy habits, excessive TV watching, or lack of physical activity. While humorous, it can also highlight concerns about sedentary lifestyles.

Related Idioms in English:

"Lazy bones" – A lazy person.

"Sit on your hands" – To remain inactive or avoid taking action.

Examples from Daily Life:

Family: "My brother is such a couch potato – he never wants to go outside and play sports."

Friends: "We were all couch potatoes during the rainy weekend, just watching movies and eating snacks."

Lifestyle: "I realized I was turning into a couch potato, so I joined a gym to get more active."

Conclusion:

The idiom "couch potato" humorously captures the image of someone overly fond of lounging and watching TV. While often playful, it also serves as a gentle reminder about the importance of balancing leisure with an active lifestyle.

Notes:

"Eat Like a Horse" – To Eat a Lot

Meaning of the Idiom:

"Eat like a horse" refers to eating large quantities of food, often in a surprising or excessive manner. The idiom describes someone with a huge appetite or someone who consumes very hearty meals.

History and Origin:

Literal Reference: The phrase draws from the image of a horse, a large animal requiring significant amounts of food daily to sustain its size and energy.

Spread of Usage: The idiom appeared in English during the 19th century and quickly gained popularity in everyday conversations, particularly in humorous contexts.

Cultural Significance: It is often used in family jokes or friendly remarks, especially to describe children or young adults with big appetites.

Examples of Usage in English:

"He eats like a horse after football practice – he's always starving!"

"I don't know where she puts it all – she eats like a horse but stays so thin."

"During the holidays, everyone in our family eats like a horse."

Cultural Context:

"Eat like a horse" is a widely used idiom in English-speaking cultures, particularly in family and social settings. The expression carries a humorous tone and is often used to emphasize someone's incredible appetite without being judgmental.

Related Idioms in English:

"Eat like a pig" – To eat a lot, sometimes in a messy way.

"Have a bottomless pit" – To have an insatiable appetite.

Examples from Daily Life:

Family: "My teenage son eats like a horse – I can barely keep the fridge stocked!"

Sports: "After a long day of training, the athletes eat like horses to regain their energy."

Social Gatherings: "At the buffet, he ate like a horse and tried almost everything on the menu."

Conclusion:

The idiom "eat like a horse" humorously captures the image of someone with a voracious appetite, often used affectionately or playfully to describe hearty eaters in various contexts.

Notes:

"Burn Your Fingers" – To Harm Yourself

Meaning of the Idiom:

"Burn your fingers" means to suffer harm or loss as a result of one's own actions, often due to overconfidence, carelessness, or engaging in risky ventures. The idiom implies that the person has learned a painful lesson to be more cautious in the future.

History and Origin:

Literal Reference: The idiom stems from the metaphor of touching something hot, which causes immediate pain and serves as a reminder to be careful.

First Usage: The phrase began appearing in English in the 19th century, initially in financial contexts and later in broader situations involving risk.

Popularity: Over time, it became widely used in literature and everyday language as a warning against rash decisions.

Examples of Usage in English:

"He burned his fingers by investing in a company without doing proper research."

"She burned her fingers by trusting someone who wasn't reliable."

"I once burned my fingers in a risky business deal – now I'm much more cautious."

Cultural Context:

"Burn your fingers" is a versatile idiom applied across various scenarios, including finance, personal relationships, and everyday life, to highlight the consequences of risky actions. It is especially common when offering advice or warning someone against repeating mistakes.

Related Idioms in English:

"Learn the hard way" – To learn something through a painful experience.

"Pay the price" – To face the consequences of one's actions.

Examples from Daily Life:

Finance: "He burned his fingers in the stock market crash and now avoids high-risk investments."

Relationships: "She burned her fingers by trusting her ex-boyfriend, who let her down again."

Career: "I burned my fingers by taking on a project without enough preparation – it was a tough lesson."

Conclusion:

The idiom "burn your fingers" serves as a vivid reminder of the potential consequences of hasty or unwise decisions. Its use underscores the importance of caution and thoughtful consideration in avoiding harm or loss.

Notes:

"Piece of Cake" – Something Very Easy

Meaning of the Idiom:

"Piece of cake" refers to something very easy to do, a task that requires little effort or skill. The phrase is often used in casual conversations to describe situations that are simple and straightforward.

History and Origin:

Culinary Reference: The expression comes from the idea of eating cake, which is enjoyable and effortless, making it a metaphor for easy tasks.

First Usage: The idiom emerged in English in the early 20th century, gaining popularity through American culture.

Modern Usage: It is widely used in informal contexts, both in professional settings and everyday conversations.

Examples of Usage in English:

"The math test was a piece of cake – I finished it in ten minutes."

"Don't worry about assembling the furniture; it's a piece of cake."

"Cooking this recipe is a piece of cake, even for beginners."

Cultural Context:

"Piece of cake" is a well-known idiom in English-speaking cultures, often used in lighthearted and informal dialogues. It highlights the ease of tasks that might seem challenging but are actually simple to accomplish.

Related Idioms in English:

"Easy as pie" – Something very simple.

"A walk in the park" – Something easy and enjoyable to do.

Examples from Daily Life:

Work: "Fixing the bug in the software was a piece of cake for the experienced developer."

School: "Learning the new vocabulary was a piece of cake for her because she loves languages."

Daily Life: "Setting up the new phone was a piece of cake thanks to the step-by-step instructions."

Conclusion:

The idiom "piece of cake" is a versatile and universally understood phrase that conveys the simplicity of tasks. Its cheerful tone makes it a popular choice for describing easy and stress-free situations.

Notes:

"Have a Lot on One's Plate" – To Be Overwhelmed with Responsibilities

Meaning of the Idiom:

"Have a lot on one's plate" means that someone has many responsibilities, tasks, or problems to deal with. The phrase is used to describe a person who feels overwhelmed or busy with various commitments.

History and Origin:

Culinary Reference: The idiom originates from the metaphor of a plate filled with food, symbolizing the amount of work or obligations someone must "consume" or handle.

Spread of Usage: The phrase began to gain popularity in the United States during the 20th century, particularly in the context of work and daily life.

Cultural Significance: It reflects modern life's fast pace and the stress associated with juggling multiple responsibilities.

Examples of Usage in English:

"I can't take on another project right now – I already have a lot on my plate."

"She has a lot on her plate with work, family, and planning her wedding."

"Don't bother him about the meeting; he's got a lot on his plate today."

Cultural Context:

"Have a lot on one's plate" is a widely used idiom in both informal and formal conversations. It is commonly applied in work environments, educational contexts, and personal life to describe someone who is busy or overwhelmed with various obligations.

Related Idioms in English:

"Up to one's ears" – To be deeply immersed in work or problems.

"Spread too thin" – To be involved in too many tasks to manage them effectively.

Examples from Daily Life:

Work: "The manager asked me to lead the new project, but I already have a lot on my plate."

Family: "She has a lot on her plate, taking care of the kids and working full-time."

Education: "With exams coming up and a part-time job, he's got a lot on his plate."

Conclusion:

The idiom "have a lot on one's plate" captures the challenges of managing multiple responsibilities in today's fast-paced world. Its relatable imagery makes it a common expression for describing busy and overwhelming situations in various aspects of life.

Notes:

"As Busy as Popcorn on a Skillet" – Extremely Busy

Meaning of the Idiom:

"As busy as popcorn on a skillet" describes being very busy, energetic, or constantly on the move, much like popcorn kernels bouncing and popping on a hot skillet. The expression emphasizes the intensity and fast pace of someone juggling multiple tasks.

History and Origin:

Literal Reference: The idiom stems from the visual image of popcorn kernels on a hot skillet, popping and moving unpredictably, symbolizing a hectic and dynamic lifestyle.

Spread of Use: This phrase is popular in American culture, particularly in informal contexts. Its vivid imagery and humorous undertone make it appealing in everyday speech.

Examples of Usage in English:

"With the kids running around and guests arriving, I felt as busy as popcorn on a skillet."

"She's as busy as popcorn on a skillet preparing for the big event tomorrow."

"He's been as busy as popcorn on a skillet trying to juggle work and family commitments."

Cultural Context:

"As busy as popcorn on a skillet" is used mainly in informal conversations to describe someone exceptionally active and busy. While it conveys a sense of productivity, it can also imply chaos or difficulty in managing responsibilities.

Related Idioms in English:

"As busy as a bee" – To be very busy and productive.

"Running around like a chicken with its head cut off" – To be busy in a chaotic or disorganized way.

Examples from Daily Life:

Family: "With three kids to look after, she's as busy as popcorn on a skillet every morning."

Work: "He's as busy as popcorn on a skillet preparing for the product launch."

Social Life: "Planning the party made me feel as busy as popcorn on a skillet – so much to do!"

Conclusion:

The idiom "as busy as popcorn on a skillet" vividly captures the energy and intensity of a busy life. Its lighthearted tone makes it a favorite in describing hectic days with humor and relatability.

Notes:

"Have a Sweet Tooth" – To Love Sweets

Meaning of the Idiom:

"Have a sweet tooth" means having a strong preference for sweet-tasting foods or desserts. The phrase describes someone who enjoys indulging in chocolates, candies, cakes, and other sugary treats.

History and Origin:

Literal Reference: The expression originates from the metaphorical association of "tooth" with taste preferences. A "sweet tooth" implies a fondness for sweet flavors.

Spread of Use: The idiom appeared in English in the 18th century and has remained a popular term for describing people who enjoy sugary foods.

Universality: A similar expression exists in many languages, reflecting the widespread love for sweets across cultures.

Examples of Usage in English:

"She has a sweet tooth and can't resist chocolate cake."

"If you have a sweet tooth, you'll love this bakery – they make amazing pastries."

"He's trying to cut back on sugar, but his sweet tooth makes it difficult."

Cultural Context:

"Have a sweet tooth" is a widely used idiom in everyday conversations, particularly when discussing food preferences or dietary habits. It carries a lighthearted and positive tone, often used humorously to describe an inclination toward desserts.

Related Idioms in English:

"Sugar rush" – A burst of energy after consuming a large amount of sugar.

"Candy lover" – Someone who adores candies and sweets.

Examples from Daily Life:

Family: "My dad has a sweet tooth, so we always buy him chocolates for his birthday."

Social Life: "Let's go for dessert – I've got a sweet tooth tonight!"

Dieting: "Having a sweet tooth makes sticking to a diet challenging for her."

Conclusion:

The idiom "have a sweet tooth" captures the universal love for sweet treats with charm and relatability. It adds a touch of warmth and humor to conversations about food and personal preferences.

Notes:

"Know Which Side Your Bread Is Buttered On" – Understand What Benefits You

Meaning of the Idiom:

"Know which side your bread is buttered on" means understanding what or who benefits you most and making decisions to maintain those advantages. The idiom emphasizes being aware of your self-interest and acting strategically to preserve or enhance it.

History and Origin:

Literal Reference: The phrase originates from the image of buttered bread, where the "buttered side" represents the preferable, advantageous option.

First Use: The idiom appeared in English in the 17th century, initially referring to knowing how to protect one's interests.

Evolution of Meaning: Over time, the idiom has been applied in professional, social, and personal contexts to highlight pragmatism and self-awareness.

Examples of Usage in English:

"She always helps her boss with extra tasks – she knows which side her bread is buttered on."

"If you want to succeed in this company, you need to know which side your bread is buttered on."

"He keeps in good standing with his biggest client because he knows which side his bread is buttered on."

Cultural Context:

"Know which side your bread is buttered on" is widely used in English-speaking cultures, especially in professional and social settings. The idiom conveys a sense of pragmatism and an understanding of personal advantage, often in a slightly humorous or self-deprecating way.

Related Idioms in English:

"Play your cards right" – Act strategically to achieve success.

"Don't bite the hand that feeds you" – Avoid harming those who support you.

Examples from Daily Life:

Work: "He never disagrees with his manager in meetings – he knows which side his bread is buttered on."

Relationships: "She keeps her best friend happy because she knows which side her bread is buttered on."

Business: "The company focuses on customer service because they know which side their bread is buttered on."

Conclusion:

The idiom "<u>know which side your bread is buttered on</u>" underscores the importance of self-awareness and strategic thinking in various aspects of life. It serves as a reminder to recognize and maintain what benefits you most.

Notes:

9. Regional Differences in Culinary Idioms

American and British Variations in Idiom Meanings

Culinary idioms in English vary depending on the region. While many expressions are understood in both cultures, their meanings, contexts, or popularity can differ between the United States and the United Kingdom. Here are a few examples:

1. "Spill the beans" – Reveal a secret

American Context: Commonly used in everyday conversations in a light, humorous tone. It often refers to accidentally revealing a surprise.

Example: "Don't spill the beans about her surprise party!"

British Context: Less commonly used in daily speech but understood as a more formal way to describe divulging a secret.

Example: "He spilled the beans about the promotion before it was officially announced."

2. "Piece of cake" – Something very easy

American Context: A popular phrase in casual conversations, often used by younger generations.

Example: "That math test was a piece of cake!"

British Context: While the idiom is understood, the alternative "easy as pie" is more frequently heard in the UK.

Example: "The quiz was easy as pie."

3. "Go bananas" – Go crazy or get excited

American Context: Commonly used to describe an intense emotional reaction, whether positive or negative.

Example: "The fans went bananas when their team scored the winning goal."

British Context: Less popular but still understood. Britons might use "go mad" instead.

Example: "The kids went mad when they saw the birthday cake."

4. "Butter someone up" – Flatter someone

American Context: Frequently used in everyday situations to suggest trying to gain something through excessive compliments.

Example: "He's buttering up the boss to get a promotion."

British Context: Widely recognized but sometimes replaced with more direct terms like "flatter."

Example: "She's flattering the teacher to get a better grade."

5. "Bring home the bacon" – Earn a living

American Context: Deeply rooted in American culture, often referring to the role of the primary breadwinner.

Example: "He works two jobs to bring home the bacon."

British Context: Understood but less commonly used; Britons may more frequently say "earn a living."

Example: "She works hard to earn a living for her family."

6. "Take the biscuit" – Be the best (or worst)

British Context: A common expression used both positively and negatively, depending on the context.

Example: "That really takes the biscuit – I can't believe he forgot again!"

American Context: Rarely used. Americans are more likely to say "takes the cake."

Example: "That excuse really takes the cake!"

7. "Cheap as chips" – Very inexpensive

British Context: A popular phrase in the UK to describe something extremely cheap.

Example: "This used car is cheap as chips!"

American Context: Uncommon or unfamiliar; Americans are more likely to say "dirt cheap."

Example: "The tickets were dirt cheap – only $5 each!"

8. "Eat humble pie" – Admit a mistake

British Context: Frequently used, especially in formal situations or texts.

Example: "After his mistake, he had to eat humble pie and apologize."

American Context: Recognized but less commonly used; Americans often say "swallow your pride."

Example: "I had to swallow my pride and admit I was wrong."

Conclusion

American and British culinary idioms often differ in subtle nuances of meaning, popularity, and usage context. Understanding these distinctions enhances cross-cultural communication and deepens one's mastery of the English language

Notes:

Examples of Culinary Idioms Unique to Different Cultures

Culinary idioms are deeply rooted in a country's traditions and customs, making many of them unique to specific cultures. They often reflect local eating habits, societal values, or ways of thinking. Here are a few examples:

1. Poland

"Nie mój cyrk, nie moje małpy" (Not my circus, not my monkeys)

Meaning: It's not my problem.

Culinary context: Although not directly related to food, this idiom reflects a Polish approach to avoiding involvement in other people's issues, similar to "it's not my cup of tea" in English.

"Co ma piernik do wiatraka?" (What does gingerbread have to do with a windmill?)

Meaning: Two things are unrelated.

Culinary context: Gingerbread, a sweet treat, contrasts with a windmill used for grinding flour, highlighting unrelated topics.

2. Japan

"Ocha wo nigosu" (お茶を濁す) (To cloud the tea)

Meaning: To evade or avoid giving a direct answer.

Culinary context: Refers to situations where a person is unclear or avoids stating their true intentions, much like tea can be "clouded" by stirring.

"Daifuku wo shiku" (大福を敷く) (Lay down the daifuku)

Meaning: To prepare something easy and convenient.

Context: Highlights the Japanese love for simplicity in planning and actions.

3. India

"Mirch masala lagana" (मिर्च मसाला लगाना) (Add chili and spices)

Meaning: To exaggerate or dramatize.

Culinary context: Indian spices are intense and vivid, making this idiom a fitting metaphor for embellishing stories.

"Roti kapda aur makaan" (रोटी कपड़ा और मकान) (Bread, clothes, and shelter)

Meaning: Basic necessities of life.

Context: Emphasizes the importance of food as the foundation of life in Indian culture.

4. Italy

"Essere come il prezzemolo" (Be like parsley)

Meaning: To be everywhere, omnipresent.

Culinary context: Parsley is one of the most frequently used herbs in Italian cuisine, symbolizing someone who appears everywhere.

"Avere le mani in pasta" (Have one's hands in the dough)

Meaning: To be involved in something.

Context: Reflects Italians' deep love for cooking, describing someone actively engaged in a task.

5. China

"Chī ròu bù tǔ gǔ tóu" (吃肉不吐骨头) (Eat meat and not spit out the bones)

Meaning: To be selfish or greedy.

Culinary context: Describes someone who takes more than they should, often at the expense of others.

"Yī shí zhòng dào" (一石重道) (Heavy rice)

Meaning: Something significant or valuable.

Context: In China, rice is a staple food, so "heavy rice" symbolizes something important.

6. United States

"Easy as pie"

Meaning: Something very easy.

Culinary context: American pie symbolizes something simple and enjoyable, akin to "a piece of cake."

"That's the way the cookie crumbles"

Meaning: That's life; you must accept it.

Context: A crumbling cookie represents situations beyond our control.

7. France

"Mettre du beurre dans les épinards" (Put butter in the spinach)

Meaning: Improve one's financial situation.

Culinary context: Butter enhances the taste of spinach, representing adding comfort or quality to life.

"Ne pas être dans son assiette" (Not be on one's plate)

Meaning: To feel unwell or be in a bad mood.

Context: Refers to someone not being in their usual state of mind.

Conclusion

Culinary idioms are deeply embedded in culture, reflecting the traditions and values of a community. Understanding these expressions not only enriches language comprehension but also provides valuable insight into the cultural differences that shape how people communicate worldwide.

How Translation Alters the Meaning of Expressions

Translating idioms is a challenging task because idioms are deeply embedded in culture and often carry meanings that are not literal. Transferring these meanings to another language can lead to:

1. Loss of Cultural Significance

Idioms often reference local customs, foods, traditions, or history that may be unfamiliar in another culture.

English idiom: "Spill the beans" (Reveal a secret).

Literal Polish translation: „Rozlać fasolę."

Problem: Poles might not associate spilling beans with revealing secrets due to the lack of cultural context. A better equivalent would be „Wygadać się" (to blurt out).

2. Change in Emotional Tone

Some idioms carry different emotional connotations in various languages.

French idiom: "Ne pas être dans son assiette" (To not feel well).

Literal translation: "Not to be on one's plate."

Problem: This literal translation sounds odd in Polish. A better equivalent would be „Nie być w formie" (not feeling well).

3. Absence of an Equivalent

Some idioms have no direct equivalent in the target language. Translators must find expressions that convey similar meaning without a direct translation.

Polish idiom: „Nie mój cyrk, nie moje małpy" (Not my circus, not my monkeys).

Literal translation: "Not my circus, not my monkeys."

English equivalent: "Not my problem."

Problem: While understandable, the literal version loses its humor, so it is often adapted.

4. Change in Meaning Due to Literal Translation

Literal translation of idioms can lead to absurd results.

English idiom: "When pigs fly" (Something that will never happen).

Literal Polish translation: „Kiedy świnie latają."

Problem: Poles more commonly say „Prędzej mi kaktus na dłoni wyrośnie" (Sooner will a cactus grow on my palm), which carries the same meaning but uses a culturally specific metaphor.

5. Adding or Losing Humor

Some idioms are humorous in one language but sound strange or overly serious in another.

American idiom: "The world is your oyster" (The world is open to you).

Problem: Literal translation „Świat jest twoją ostrygą" loses both its humor and clarity in cultures where oysters do not carry metaphorical significance.

6. Lack of Cultural Context in the Target Language

Certain idioms are incomprehensible without cultural context.

Japanese idiom: "Kaeru no ko wa kaeru" (A frog's child is a frog – children resemble their parents).

Problem: In Polish culture, frogs do not symbolize generational continuity. A better equivalent is „Niedaleko pada jabłko od jabłoni" (The apple doesn't fall far from the tree).

Translation Strategies for Idioms

Replace with a Local Equivalent

Example: "Bite the bullet" (Endure something painful) → „Zacisnąć zęby" (Grit one's teeth).

Descriptive Translation

Example: "Break the ice" → „Rozpocząć rozmowę w niezręcznej sytuacji" (Start a conversation in an awkward situation).

Retain the Idiom in its Original Form

This can work if the context allows understanding or if the idiom is globally recognized.

Use a Neutral Phrase

If the idiom is too challenging to translate, replace it with a straightforward sentence.

Conclusion

Translating idioms requires not only linguistic knowledge but also cultural understanding and awareness of the author's intent. Adapting idioms to the target language preserves their meaning, tone, and emotion while making the message clear and natural for the audience.

Notes:

10. Quiz: What Does This Idiom Mean?

Test your knowledge of culinary idioms by taking this quiz. Choose the correct meaning for each idiom. Answers are provided at the end.

1. "Spill the beans"

A. Spill a drink.

B. Reveal a secret.

C. Clean the kitchen.

D. Prepare a meal.

2. "Piece of cake"

A. A slice of cake.

B. Something very difficult.

C. Something very easy.

D. A pleasant surprise.

3. "Butter someone up"

A. Spread butter on bread.

B. Flatter someone to get something.

C. Confuse someone.

D. Prepare something with butter.

4. "Have bigger fish to fry"

A. Have more important things to do.

B. Prepare a large meal.

C. Catch bigger fish.

D. Do something for show.

5. "Cry over spilled milk"

A. Worry about something that can't be changed.

B. Be sad because of failure.

C. Complain about the taste of milk.

D. Spill milk and clean it up.

6. "Take with a grain of salt"

A. Take something with skepticism.

B. Improve something with seasoning.

C. Disagree with something.

D. Add salt to a meal.

7. "Full of beans"

A. Have a lot of work.

B. Be full of energy.

C. Be absent-minded.

D. Be malicious.

8. "As cool as a cucumber"

A. Be very calm and composed.

B. Be cold as ice.

C. Be bored.

D. Be rude.

9. "Out to lunch"

A. Be out for lunch.

B. Be mentally absent.

C. Be preparing food.

D. Refuse to eat.

10. "Burn your fingers"

A. Harm yourself through your own actions.

B. Cook something hot.

C. Be reckless.

D. Burn yourself while cooking.

Answers

1.B Reveal a secret

2.C Something very easy

3.B Flatter someone to get something

4.A Have more important things to do

5.A Worry about something that can't be changed

6.A Take something with skepticism

7.B Be full of energy

8.A Be very calm and composed

9.B Be mentally absent

10.A Harm yourself through your own actions

10. Tips for Using Idioms in Everyday Conversation

Using idioms in daily conversations can enrich your language, making your speech more engaging and natural. However, their effective use requires appropriate context and understanding. Here are some practical tips:

1. Understand the idiom's meaning

Before using an idiom, ensure you fully understand its figurative meaning. Idioms often carry meanings that aren't immediately clear from the words themselves.

Example:

"Break the ice" – It means to start a conversation in an awkward situation, not literally breaking ice.

2. Use idioms in the right context

Idioms are most effective when they fit the situation naturally. Avoid forcing them into conversations if they don't align with the topic.

Example:

"Spill the beans" (Reveal a secret) works when discussing surprises but not in a formal workplace report.

3. Match idioms to your audience

Consider whether the person you're speaking with will understand the idiom. Some idioms are specific to certain cultures or regions. If speaking with someone for whom English is not the first language, opt for more universal expressions.

Example:

Instead of "When pigs fly" (Something that will never happen), say "That will never happen."

4.Avoid overusing idioms

Using too many idioms can make your speech feel artificial or confusing. Incorporate them sparingly as a way to enhance, not dominate, your conversation.

Example:

Use one or two idioms in a short conversation, no more.

5.Practice with popular idioms

Start with commonly used idioms that are easy to understand and applicable in various situations.

Examples of popular idioms:

"Piece of cake" – Something very easy.

"A blessing in disguise" – Something that seems bad but turns out good.

"The ball is in your court" – It's your decision to make.

6.Adapt to the tone and formality of the conversation

Idioms are more suitable for informal settings, such as conversations with friends, family, or colleagues in casual contexts. In formal situations, opt for straightforward language.

Example:

Informal: "Let's break the ice before we start the meeting."

Formal: "Let's start with a brief introduction to make everyone comfortable."

7. Learn idioms in context

Memorize idioms by studying examples of their use in context. This will help you understand their meaning and learn how to use them correctly.

Example:

Read books, watch movies, or listen to podcasts where idioms are used naturally.

8. Be ready to explain idioms

If you use an idiom and your listener doesn't understand, be prepared to explain it. Offer a simple explanation in the language you're both communicating in.

Example:

Idiom: "To hit the nail on the head."

Explanation: "It means to describe something exactly right."

9. Use idioms to express emotions

Idioms can add flair to your emotional expressions.

Example:

Instead of: "I'm very happy."

Say: "I'm on cloud nine."

10. Experiment and be open to feedback

Using idioms might feel challenging at first, but practice makes perfect. Don't be afraid to make mistakes; over time, it will feel more natural. If someone

Idioms add character and vibrancy to conversations, but using them effectively requires thoughtfulness and practice. Be patient, and remember that mastering each new expression makes your communication more engaging and authentic!

Acknowledgments and Announcement of Upcoming Books in the Series

Acknowledgments

At the end of this book, I want to express my heartfelt gratitude to everyone who supported me throughout its creation. Your curiosity, passion for learning, and interest in idioms made working on this project an absolute joy.

I am deeply thankful to my family, friends, and mentors, whose encouragement and motivation have been invaluable. Your suggestions, feedback, and unwavering support have helped make this book more engaging and enriching.

A special thank you goes to my readers – your love for language and desire to embrace new challenges inspire me to create content that educates and motivates.

Announcement of Upcoming Books

This book is part of a series dedicated to fascinating idioms and their meanings. In upcoming publications, I invite you to explore even more intriguing expressions and their surprising backstories.

Coming Soon in the Series:

1."Idioms That Surprise Us: Animal Expressions and Their Stories"

A dive into idioms inspired by animals and their metaphorical meanings.

2."Idioms That Surprise Us: Food Expressions Around the World"

Culinary idioms from different cultures – their meanings and cultural contexts.

3."Idioms That Surprise Us: Everyday Expressions for Success"

Phrases perfect for conversations at work, school, and in everyday interactions.

4."Idioms That Surprise Us: Funny and Strange Expressions"

The most humorous and peculiar idioms guaranteed to entertain every reader.

Final Note

I hope this series becomes a source of inspiration and a delightful way for you to learn the language. If you have ideas for new topics or would like to share your thoughts, feel free to reach out!

Thank you for reading, and I look forward to seeing you in the next book!

Made in the USA
Monee, IL
03 May 2026

49438706R00089